AND GOD CAME IN

HENDRICKSON CLASSIC BIOGRAPHIES

Roland H. Bainton, *Here I Stand:*
A Life of Martin Luther

G. K. Chesterton, *Saint Francis of Assisi*

Charles Colson, *Born Again*

Fanny J. Crosby, *Fanny J. Crosby:*
An Autobiography

Lyle W. Dorsett, *And God Came In:*
The Extraordinary Story of Joy Davidman

Elisabeth Elliot, *Shadow of the Almighty:*
The Life and Testament of Jim Elliot

Percy Livingston Parker (editor),
The Heart of John Wesley's Journal

Arthur T. Pierson, *George Müller of Bristol*

Howard and Geraldine Taylor,
Hudson Taylor's Spiritual Secret

Corrie ten Boom, with Elizabeth and John Sherrill,
The Hiding Place

AND GOD CAME IN

The Extraordinary Story of Joy Davidman

Her Life and Marriage to C. S. Lewis

LYLE W. DORSETT

A HENDRICKSON CLASSIC BIOGRAPHY

And God Came In

Hendrickson Publishers Marketing, LLC
P. O. Box 3473
Peabody, Massachusetts 01961-3473

ISBN: 978-1-59856-356-6

Printed in the United States of America

First Hendrickson Edition Printing—June 2009

All photographs used by permission of The Marion E. Wade Center, Wheaton College, Wheaton, IL.

　　　　Library of Congress Cataloging-in-Publication Data
Dorsett, Lyle W.
　And God came in : the extraordinary story of Joy Davidman / Lyle W. Dorsett.—Hendrickson classic biographies ed.
　　p. cm.
　Includes index.
　ISBN 978-1-59856-356-6 (alk. paper)
1. Davidman, Joy. 2. Christian converts from Judaism—United States—Biography. 3. Authors' spouses—Great Britain—Biography. 4.Lewis, C. S. (Clive Staples), 1898-1963—Marriage. I. Title.
　BV2623.D38D67 2009
　283.092—dc22
　[B]
　　　　　　　　　2009008754

To Albert George (Bert) and
Mary Greco Hayes
with Love

*I must say I was the
world's most surprised atheist.*

Joy Davidman
New York Post,
November 10, 1949

Contents

Preface to the

Hendrickson Classic Biographies

Edition

I t is an honor and privilege to have *And God Came In* as part of Hendrickson's classic biographies series. It not only encourages me as the book's author to see the book "Revived," so to speak, but it is especially pleasing to know that the true story of Joy Davidman, particularly her years with C. S. Lewis, will be offered to the public in an exciting new format. To be sure, this brilliant American novelist, poet, and critic is no longer obscure like she was before *And God Came In* first appeared more than a quarter century ago. Nevertheless, Joy Davidman, if not unknown, needs to be rescued from the utterly false images of her that have appeared in two *Shadowlands* films. Both movies relied heavily upon my research and writing, but in both films the producers and screenplay writers distorted important facts for dramatic effect and for purposes of promoting their own biases. Joy, for instance, never begged C. S. Lewis to marry her so that she could remain living in England. On the contrary, Lewis insisted on the marriage rather than see her deported to America. Furthermore, when Joy suffered from a dreadfully advanced case of cancer, the lengthy and unexpected remission, according to her physician, resulted primarily from the healing prayer of an Anglican priest, Father Peter Bide, not as a consequence of the radiation therapy depicted in the film. In the same fictional vein the motion picture shows C. S. Lewis devastated and nearly robbed of his faith when Joy's cancer returns with a vengeance and causes her death. But letters Professor Lewis wrote after Joy's death, as well as testimony of several of his friends, reveal that his faith and courage survived in robust fashion.

I am deeply grateful for the advent of this new edition of the Joy Davidman story. It is my earnest prayer the reader will find that the true story of Joy's life is much more interesting and God glorifying than the story that the fictional films offer.

Lyle W. Dorsett
January 2009

PREFACE TO THE 1982 EDITION

There was absolutely nothing ordinary about Joy Davidman Lewis. Her IQ was unusually high; her memory nearly photographic. She read H. G. Wells's *Outline of History* at age eight and promptly announced her atheism. A voracious reader, ready for college by age fourteen, Joy postponed matriculation until the following year. Graduation from Hunter College came at nineteen; Joy was awarded a master's degree at Columbia University three semesters later. During the depression of the 1930s, Joy Davidman grew disillusioned with the American economic system and joined the Communist Party. After teaching high school for two years, she experimented with scriptwriting in Hollywood. By 1940 the twenty-five-year-old dynamo was serving on the staff of a weekly magazine and, in addition to editing a book of poetry, had published a poetry book of her own as well as a novel and numerous pieces in magazines.

The Davidman family was Jewish, but socialism and rationalism—not Judaism—comprised their religion. The first in a series of disappointments to Joy's family came in 1942 when she married William Lindsay Gresham. Not only a gentile and a Southerner, he was also an impoverished freelance writer who supplemented his income singing folk songs in Greenwich Village nightclubs. Although Joy's family was delighted when she gave birth to two healthy sons, they were dismayed in 1947 when she embraced Christianity and was baptized.

The new Christian had a knack for astounding people. If her Jewish relatives were stunned by her marriage and conversion, her literary colleagues were perplexed by the fact that she published only one more novel, turning from writing fiction and poetry to Christian apologetics. Finally she angered some of the Anglican world and bewildered all when she moved to England, and, after her divorce, married celebrated bachelor C. S. Lewis.

Joy Davidman continued to shock people until the day she died. Doctors had pronounced her cancer incurable. Near what was assumed to be the end, physicians gave her only days to live. But the plucky and unpredictable woman emerged from her bed, made of Lewis a happy husband, traveled to Ireland and Greece, and began work on another book.

I decided to write a biography of this most remarkable woman because her story needs to be told. Not only has there been no one to step forward and write about her life, the little that is known about her is obscured by the shadow of C. S. Lewis. Joy Davidman Lewis had a full and fascinating life before she ever met the renowned writer. Furthermore, she was markedly more important to him than their brief time together might suggest.

Her story must be told because it glorifies God rather than herself or C. S. Lewis. Joy was not a saintly person. Few people remember her as being particularly righteous. She most certainly did not appear pious. The point is that for over three decades she was a tortured soul who sought fulfillment in numerous places— to no avail. After her encounter with Christ, Joy did experience meaning, direction, happiness, and eventually peace of mind. She did not *find* these riches; they were a *gift* from God.

What is notable about Joy's life is not that she was imperfect after conversion; the significance of her life is that she did grow into spiritual maturity. To be sure, her old nemesis, self-will, emerged from time to time; more than one person was the victim of her volatile temper and acerbic tongue. Nevertheless, as she allowed Jesus to become the Lord of her life, he changed her and he was able to use her in strikingly important ways. There is a lesson here for us.

L. W. D.

September 1982

Acknowledgments
and Sources

The sources for this book are unusually rich. A number of Joy's friends granted me lengthy and candid interviews. Several people in the United States were especially helpful to me. In Vermont I talked with Joy's good friends the Walshes, Eva and Chad; in New York Dr. Howard Davidman, Joy's brother, shared two afternoons with me; and in Florida I twice visited Mrs. William Lindsay (Renée) Gresham, Joy's first cousin. In England I benefited from generous talks with Professor George Sayer, Miss Jean Wakeman, the Reverend Walter Hooper, and the Reverend R. E. Head.

Nearly a score of Joy's college classmates, former students, and writing colleagues have corresponded or talked with me on the telephone. Joy's two sons, Douglas Gresham of Tasmania, Australia, and David Gresham of Switzerland, have shared memories with me as well.

Special thanks go to Professor Chad Walsh, who read the manuscript, made helpful suggestions, and gave me permission to use his photographs. My parents, Eda and Al Dorsett, read an early draft and offered useful criticisms. Salome Breck, our Denver friend, generously took several photographs in London and Oxford for this book. I am also indebted to Alexia Dorszynski, my editor at Macmillan, for all her assistance.

Finally, I owe an immeasurable debt to my wife. She helped with the research, did all the typing, and served as an invaluable critic. Her love and prayers made this book possible.

Although all of the people mentioned here have helped me with this book, not every one of them will share my interpretations. I also assume full responsibility for all errors.

Materials relating to Joy Davidman are in the C. S. Lewis Papers housed in the Marion E. Wade Collection at Wheaton College. Especially helpful to me were Evelyn Brace, Clyde S. Kilby, Marjorie Mead, Stephen Parker, Brenda Blount Phillips, and Peter Veltman. Although there are references to Joy in the Wade Collection, none of her own papers were there until 1982. In May 1981 I discovered that Renée Gresham, the widow of William Lindsay Gresham, lives in Florida. She had all her husband's papers as well as over five hundred letters to and from Joy Davidman and her sons. Likewise several heretofore undiscovered C. S. Lewis letters, and many photographs of him and the boys, were among these things. Renée Gresham generously allowed me permission to copy and use these papers and photographs. Furthermore, she granted me several days of interviews. Her reminiscences were quite valuable inasmuch as she was Joy's first cousin and was well acquainted with the Davidman family. Renée married William Lindsay Gresham after Gresham and Joy were divorced. Thanks to leads from Renée and Chad Walsh, I have uncovered several other small collections of materials relating to Joy Davidman. All these letters and documents are now in the Marion E. Wade Collection.

In brief, 95 percent of this biography is based upon hitherto untapped primary sources. To learn precisely what sources I have relied upon for each portion of the text, the reader should consult the Notes at the end of the book.

Chapter 1

EMBATTLED PRODIGY
(1915–1934)

"I Heard the Voice in the Burning Bush"

It was a cold, clear Sunday afternoon in New York City. The year was 1929. Fourteen-year-old Joy Davidman was walking through the park and enjoying the snow that had fallen a few hours before. The strange quiet that accompanies a snowfall made the sunset hour enchanting, especially when she looked at the row of ice-clad maple trees that stood between her and the lowering sun. "As I looked up they burned unimaginably golden—burned and were not consumed. I heard the voice in the burning tree: the meaning of all things was revealed and the sacrament at the heart of all beauty lay bare; time and space fell away, and for a moment the world was only a door swinging ajar,"[1] she was to write—later.

This was not Joy's first mystical experience, and it wouldn't be her last. For an instant she believed that she had entered a spiritual realm as real as the material world so familiar around her. But the cold wind on her face and her reflex recollection of her father's admonitions against any such conclusion, brought her mind back to the mundane. She shrugged off her response as the glandular reaction of a sensitive person upon encountering unusual beauty. Beautiful things just did that to people. Science had not explained it yet, but it would one day. "I went home, reflecting that I had had another aesthetic experience. I had them fairly often. . . . For I was a well-brought-up, right-thinking child of materialism. Beauty, I knew, existed; but God, of course, did not."[2]

If most American children grow up in homes where God is worshiped, or at least indifferently assumed to exist, then Joy Davidman's upbringing was out of the mainstream. Although her mother made perfunctory nods in the direction of the Judaism of her birth and attempted to preserve the forms of faith, Joy's father was an outspoken atheist who exhorted others in his household to share his view. Joy actually grew up in a family where religion was at once respected and deplored. The faith of her ancestors could not be ignored; nevertheless, whatever attitude Joy adopted toward the religion of the Old World seemed to invite criticism.

Helen Joy Davidman (everyone called her Joy) was born into a family where battles over religion were inevitable. Both sets of grandparents immigrated to the United States in the late nineteenth century, part of the great migration of southern and eastern Europeans who entered America during the years between the 1880s and World War I. These were the so-called new immigrants, "new" because they were from the south and east of Europe rather than from the north and west, where most earlier American immigrant movements originated. These "new" Americans were different from most previous settlers because they were predominantly Jewish and Roman Catholic, rather than Protestant. Approximately 80,000 Jews, most of western European origin, lived in New York in 1870. They comprised less than 10 percent of the population. By 1915, the year of Joy Davidman's birth, nearly 1.4 million Jewish persons lived in the great metropolis; and they totaled almost 28 percent of the population. Most of these new-comers were from eastern Europe.[3]

Both of Joy's parents were part of this great migration. Her father, Joseph Isaac Davidman, was born in Poland in 1887. He arrived in New York with his parents, brothers, and sisters in 1893. Joseph Davidman's father left Poland because most of the Jewish people there, as in other parts of eastern Europe, were either ban-ished or trampled upon by religious persecutors. The elder David-man brought his family to New York, where they resided on Manhattan's Lower East Side. At first a peddler with a pushcart, he eventually found work as a clothes presser in the garment district. Joy's grandfather reveled in America's free religious environment: he not only maintained a kosher home, but worshiped regularly and observed all traditional Jewish holy days. He died when he was only forty-eight, falling victim to pneumonia—the result of preaching in the streets, trying to convert Christians to Judaism.[4]

It was in an Orthodox family, then, that Joy's father grew up. Religion was central in the Davidman home, even after the father died. But despite Joseph's mother's attempts to keep her four boys and three girls in the fold of traditional Judaism, New York's diver-sity influenced their home as it did the homes of most Old World immigrants. The children wanted to grow up and fit into the dom-inant population. To be accepted, to earn money, and to get ahead were the young people's goals; achieving these aims often required shedding ethnic traditions.

Holding tightly to Old World religious and social traditions in a dynamic New World city seemed to be a prescription for failure in the eyes of many young Jews. If one did not choose to become completely "Americanized," only a good education or a revamped economic system could promise a better future. As social scientist Nathan Glazer observed, summing up the changes affecting America's East European Jews in the late nineteenth and early twentieth century, "they might abandon the practice of Jewish religion, but this was less conversion than the embrace of an alternative secular faith—socialism or rationalism, say, which often seemed to the outside world as Jewish as Judaism itself."[5]

Glazer's description fits Joseph Isaac Davidman. He turned his back on his parents' religion and set out to improve himself through education, and to improve his lot and that of his fellow Jews through socialism. Always a hard worker, he earned enough to pay his way through New York's City College, where he was to entertain seriously thoughts of socialism and atheism. After college Joseph became a public school teacher, and later a junior high school principal.

The woman he married came from a similar but not identical background. Jeannette Spivack's parents were Jewish, too, but in the Old World they were much better off financially than the Davidmans had been. Family lore maintains that Jeannette's father was a prosperous merchant. A native of a village near Odessa in the Ukraine, he was allowed to travel on business throughout Russia, a freedom not always extended to Jews. Although the Spivacks were relatively well established in the land of Czar Alexander, they decided to forfeit what they had for the promise of a better life in America and they immigrated to New York when Jeannette was five. In particular, Joy's grandfather was concerned about education. Because he always was a feminist he chose to go to the United States so that his girls could have access to institutions of higher learning, a privilege that would be denied them in Russia.

Jeannette Spivack's father and mother were not spiritual people. As Jeannette saw it, some Jews prayed and others fought. She was proud that her father was a fighter. Although he was not hostile to Judaism, he maintained a tepid indifference to it throughout his life. Instead of religion, his interests were business, secular education, and social activism. To these things, particularly things of the mind, he devoted his energy, time, and talent. Jeannette, therefore, was brought up in a fashion that enabled her to be comfortable with a secular—even atheist—Jew just as long as he was an intellectual with a social conscience.[6]

In 1909 the bright and petite Jeannette Spivack married Joseph Davidman. They had much in common. She, too, had earned a degree from the City College of New York and was pursuing a teaching career in the public schools. They both loved books, venerated education, saw socialism as the hope for tomorrow, and were desirous of upward mobility. Jeannette preferred to preserve the forms of Judaism for the sake of tradition, although she was neither spiritual nor pious, and while Joseph was slightly annoyed by his wife's traditionalism, he never made an issue of it because he would have alienated too many people. Had his father been alive Joseph's professed atheism would have devastated him; as it was, it disconcerted his mother and his mother-in-law, and it was sometimes irritating to his more conservative wife, who appreciated and sometimes romanticized the ways of the Old World.[7]

Their differing views on Judaism notwithstanding, the newlyweds were in agreement in enough other ways to be well suited to each other. The Davidmans worked hard and saved from their earnings. Soon they climbed out of the Manhattan ghetto, and like many upwardly mobile Jews from Eastern Europe, moved to the Bronx, the event symbolizing their arrival as members of the solid middle class. Secure in a more open and attractive neighborhood, Jen and Joe, as they were known to friends and relatives, made plans for a family. Helen Joy was their firstborn. She arrived on April 18, 1915. Howard, Joy's only sibling, was born four years later.

New York City was a tumultuous place when Joy Davidman was born. The strain of change was everywhere evident as trucks and automobiles competed with carts and buggies, and electric

streetcars gradually replaced the horse-drawn variety. Some of the
great city's streets were paved, but all thoroughfares were generously covered with horse droppings. The fashionable avenues
were equipped with street lamps, and the better buildings displayed awnings of variegated shapes and colors. The Great War
had cut immigration to a trickle, but hundreds of thousands of
people still jostled one another as they struggled for survival and
advantage. Factories consumed people as quickly as they dis-
charged pollutants. Much of the urban giant was noisy, dirty, and
dangerous; yet it continued to attract newcomers from rural and
small-town America with inducements of excitement, novelty,
anonymity, and economic opportunity.

As Joy grew up in the Bronx, she was far away from the con-
gestion and roar of the metropolis. The Woodlawn section, where
she spent her early childhood, was pastoral in comparison to most
of the city. When she was small "it possessed the quality of a bit
of forgotten country in the city. You could still find rabbit tracks in
the snow, and there was an old-fashioned orchard with blue creep-
ing myrtle under the trees." One woman of this era had fond
memories of the area where Joy grew up, noting that "for entertainment we would walk over a bridge every Sunday where there
were cows in the open air. This was the Bronx. The place was like
an island."[8] Even after the Davidmans moved to a more prestigious address near the Grand Concourse, the neighborhood was
open, clean, uncongested, and safe.

From one angle of vision Joy's childhood was idyllic. Her parents were happily married; they were always comfortable financially. Even during the Great Depression, both Davidmans were
employed, and no one ever went hungry. Furthermore, Joy and
her brother got along beautifully. Not only was she well-fed,
-clothed, and -housed, Joy was given what all well-brought-up
young girls in that era expected—a piano and several years of

lessons. Besides providing the piano—a baby grand—Joy's mother taught her to cook well, and her parents gave her an education steeped in classical music, history, and good literature.

For a young family in the 1920s and 1930s, the Davidmans were unusually well traveled. During summers, when Joseph and Jeannette enjoyed two months' vacation, the foursome went to the West Coast, visiting California, Washington state, even Vancouver, British Columbia. On one trip they took in the Grand Canyon; other summers were spent in New England. The Davidmans especially enjoyed Maine, and for several years they went to Crescent Lake in Casco, Maine. Thirty miles north of the coast at Portland, Crescent Lake is about twenty-five miles from the New Hampshire line. During World War I, Joseph planted a "victory garden" at their summer place; because everyone in the family eventually enjoyed this enterprise, arrangements were made with a local caretaker to till the soil and work in some fertilizer each spring so that when the Davidmans returned, the plot of ground was ready for sowing. They seldom missed a summer even if they went west.

Joy and Howard loved to read, and they were encouraged to do so. Although there was a decent library in their spacious, well-furnished apartment, the family book collection was not enough for the Davidman children. Howard recalled that they frequently went to the public library. During the summer, if they were not out of town, they went almost every day. The librarian would allow them only six selections each, and if they were involved in a topic or author that they felt required more than twelve volumes, the two would go to another branch library, check out a dozen more monographs, and go home to master the subject. The only problem was that sometimes they returned the borrowed items to the wrong libraries.[9]

Even as a child Joy liked the humanities, reading widely in history, philosophy, American and English literature. Her preference did not run to Henry James or John Galsworthy, both of whom were too stuffy for her taste, but she did enjoy James Branch Cabell as a stylist. By the time Joy was fourteen and ready for college, she was exceptionally well informed. After all, she had been reading since the age of two and a half or three, and the photographic memory to which everyone who knew her well attests, enabled her to retain things in a most extraordinary manner. Her brother noted that she could peruse a page of a Shakespeare play once and have it memorized.[10]

Besides the youthful pleasures of reading, gardening, and traveling, Joy and Howard shared a love for the zoo. The siblings sought diversion from hours of study by walking to the Bronx Park Zoo and talking to the animals. Since Joy, typically, was unable to maintain an ordinary appetite for an enterprise once she found it to her liking, she required more involvement with the animals than regular viewing rules and regulations permitted. Consequently, by the age of fourteen or fifteen Joy was off on nighttime adventures. Because Howard adored his sister and viewed her as his teacher, he dutifully tagged along to the zoo after its closing hours for some nocturnal encounters with the big cats. Joy wanted to get acquainted with the large felines, rather than view them from a distance. Armed with her most charming manners, the aggressive teenager coaxed the lions to the bars, petted their heads, and fed them chocolate. Apparently the lions, as well as Joy and Howard, enjoyed the after-dark visitations, because these escapades continued without incident for a long time.[11]

From one viewpoint, then, the years of Joy's youth were delightful. However, those who attribute significance to the quality and quantity of love and care given an infant might see the beginnings of another thread—far from stable and pleasant—in the first few months of Joy's life. Her mother had an unusually difficult time with Joy's birth. After the exhausting delivery, Jen took her physician's advice about the necessity of an extended period of rest, and soon after leaving the hospital, she went to a dude ranch to recover. Several weeks of fresh air in a bucolic setting restored Jen's health but deprived Joy of her mother's love and care for many weeks. Although Joseph cared for the infant during this time, Joy never became close to her father.[12]

In fact, Joy's relationship with her father was dreadful. At his best, Joe could be difficult because, as one grandson put it, "He was sadly lacking in sense of humor, and was stingy about money"[13]—an assessment corroborated by his son and niece. At his worst, Joseph could be a martinet.[14] His niece, Renée, was taken aback to find her Uncle Joe summoning his children with a metal whistle. She was appalled by the way Joy and Howard ran to him in the fashion of trained dogs as soon as the whistle was blown.

Renée, whose mother was Joseph Davidman's sister, would have been more horrified still if she had seen how her cousins were disciplined. Joseph was incredibly demanding; nothing less than perfection was tolerated in his house. He was demanding of himself, too. Indeed, his reputation—which he himself promulgated—was one of never failing or making mistakes. His grades in school and college had been excellent, his teaching outstanding, and his administration of school and home flawlessly efficient. Only once did anyone ever catch him in failure! He and a fellow teacher began a summer camp for New York children, and the venture was a fiasco. Joe salvaged his reputation by blaming the loss totally on the ineptitude of his partner.[15]

This man, who pushed himself to achieve, put great pressure on his children. While they were still young, Joseph Davidman brought IQ tests home from his junior high school and administered them to Howard and Joy. A score of 140 or more was undisputedly in the genius category, and although Howard scored nearly 150, his father was not pleased. The lad was told he would never amount to much. Howard's dream was to become a physician, an ambition realized when he graduated from medical school in 1943. He had received no encouragement from his father, who told him that he was not bright enough for so rigorous an academic program. Nevertheless, Howard tried to please Joseph. Because Joseph liked and taught biology, Howard took up entomology, hoping to win approval from his father. Likewise, when Jen wanted Howard to become a bar mitzvah at age thirteen, the boy sided with his father and proclaimed himself an atheist. To Joseph's delight the issue was dropped when Howard said that he would announce his atheism to the rabbi and everyone else present if he were forced to take part in the ceremony.[16]

Jeannette, as a rule, treated Howard extremely well; while he was a child, mother and son were quite close. And Joy and Howard were close friends as youngsters. They went places together, read many of the same books, and defended one another against all comers; Joseph's harsh and demanding behavior toward them both did much to bind them together. Not until adulthood would they have a serious falling out.

While Howard had scored a mere 147 on the IQ test, Joy virtually, broke the scale. This brought a smile to her father's face, but it meant that he would push her unmercifully to excel in all things.[17]

The pressure to perform at peak level never let up. Even mealtime was devoted to discussions of weighty subjects, rather than light and loving family chatter. Because the perfect father could never be wrong, and because Joy was driven to be perfect, too, there was no way that she and her father could take opposite sides on an issue and leave it at that; agreement to disagree was out of the question. Inevitably, discussions evolved into arguments, and arguments eventually led to long-lasting resentments. To make matters even worse, when Joseph Davidman grew angry with Joy for disobedience, he would hold her by the nape of the neck and forcefully slap her face several times. This punishment was used on both Howard and Joy for years, and it did not end for Howard until he went away to college. For Joy, however, it ended when she was sixteen. One evening when her father began slapping her, Joy went on the attack, ferociously scratching his face. The stunned disciplinarian never laid hands on her again.[18]

Although Joy's mother was soft-spoken and full of good humor—a raconteuse generally well-liked by everyone—she, too, could be cruel to Joy. Renée saw Aunt Jen as a neat, pretty, and charming woman who was almost prissy. She possessed the soft voice that is acquired by so many kindergarten and first-grade teachers. While Jen was unquestionably kind to her niece, she had a tendency to denigrate other people. Howard was to say that she used subtle sarcasm to insult people, saying a person was "pedestrian," then apologizing and saying she really meant to say "protestant." But the brunt of her snideness was reserved for Joy. Renée blushed with embarrassment when Aunt Jen would say, "Joy, why can't you be neat like your cousin?" Or "Look at Renée, this is how a *lady* should look in her clothes."[19]

Despite Joy's problems with her father, she, too, made herculean efforts to win his praise, wanting confirmation of his approval. She read what he liked, and then sought to impress him with her recall and insights. Because he was a thorough materialist, believing everything can be explained through the existence and nature of matter, she read H. G. Wells's *Outline of History*, proudly telling her father that, like him and Wells, she was now an atheist. She was eight at the time.[20] She announced at age twelve that she wanted to become a writer; this pleased her father, too. And the enthusiasm with which she approached gardening allowed some pleasant times for the two of them. Joy's commitment to intellectual respectability, her celebration of reason as the only

means to discern truth, and her love for gardening and writing satisfied her father as much as anyone could. Wistfully, Howard
recalled that in those particulars, Joy had become the son Joseph
always wanted.

Regardless of the victories that came in the battles to win
Joseph's favor and occasional applause, there was continual tension
in the Davidman household. The arguments never ceased, the pressure to be perfect never lessened, and the fear of harsh discipline
was always present. Fear, in short, was a constant companion.

There was another source of anxiety swirling about the entire
Davidman family. As Jews, they were always pursued by the
demons of anti-Semitism. A look here, an insult there—it never
really stopped. It was worse when a vacation was planned. There
was invariably the threat of their being denied accommodations if
they strayed too far from the safe places of the familiar Northeast.
But anti-Semitism was rampant even in New York with its sizable
Jewish population. As Joy's gentile sister-in-law commented many
years later, "You cannot understand Howard and Joy without
some comprehension of the wickedness of anti-Semitism in New
York City."[21]

This problem took on major proportions when it came to
finding employment or gaining access to good colleges and uni-
versities. Perhaps these realities place Joseph Davidman's demanding character in a slightly more favorable light. After all, he knew
it would be more difficult for his children to get ahead because
they were Jewish. They would have to strive harder than and be
superior to gentiles in order to have a chance in a militantly com-
petitive society where people used every advantage, even if it
meant resorting to bigotry.

Added to the trials of family and prejudice were Joy's considerable physical illnesses. As a little girl, Joy would go to bed in

pain. But annoying as they were, it was not the leather curlers that her mother insisted on putting in her hair every night that hurt her; but a crooked spine, which was not properly diagnosed for several years.[22] Joy also suffered from a severe case of Grave's disease. This condition, known also as hyperthyroidism or exophthalmic goiter, is an overactive thyroid problem that causes among other things, protruding eyes. Joy's hyperthyroidism was misdiagnosed for a long time; when it was finally pinpointed, surgery was prescribed to remove part of the thyroid. The threat of surgery was removed, however, when the family found a physician who was experimenting with a radium treatment. His plan was to place a radium belt around the patient's neck for twenty-four hours once a week for an entire year. He theorized that the radioactivity would be absorbed by the thyroid gland, suppressing its hyperactivity.

Fearful of surgery, Joy submitted to this therapy almost gleefully. The treatment was an apparent success: her hyperthyroidism was cured. In retrospect, however, the cure was certainly worse than the disease. Joy's body was riddled with cancer soon after she turned forty, and many physicians see a direct cause-and-effect relationship between exposure to radium and cancer.

Grave's disease and curvature of the spine were not Joy's only medical problems. She suffered from hyperinsulinism as well. Hyperinsulinism, or excessive insulin secretion, results in a low level of sugar in the blood. Effects of this condition can include tremors, cold sweats, and an enormous appetite. Joy was subject to fainting spells and had an insatiable appetite. Joy's weight increased and to keep her from yielding to the constant temptation to eat, Jeannette had a lock installed on the refrigerator. Only after a period of scoldings, embarrassment, and confusion was Joy's actual condition diagnosed.[23]

While in high school Joy suffered a severe case of scarlet fever. This ailment kept her out of classes for six months. No sooner had she recovered from this problem than she was laid low by anemia, and once again missed school for extended periods of time.[24]

Bouts with disease brought pain and sorrow into Joy's young life, but her ailments were mild compared with her lonely inner struggle. Her father always insisted that a person with intellectual respectability was a materialist. The spiritual world was not even elevated, in his eyes, to the level of active imagination. On the contrary, people who pursued truth and reality in the realm of the unseen were, like medieval people, ignorant and superstitious. While growing up Joy wanted, above all, to be intellectually respectable and admired by her father. Thus she embraced his materialistic philosophy without question. Later, she was to say "[We] sucked in atheism with [our] canned milk. We hardly thought about it at all, and most of us were no less religious than many churchgoers."[25]

Nevertheless, Joy had to be true to herself. In quiet moments, alone with her thoughts, she had to admit that her emotions and desires told her that there was much more to this life than matter and energy. Joy noted that, "underneath the surface my own real personality stirred, stretched its wings, discovered its own tastes. It was a girl with vague eyes, who scribbled verses—scribbled them in blind fury, not knowing what she wrote or why and read them afterwards with wonder." She said that worldings call such creativity "poetic inspiration," but it might more accurately be labeled "prophecy."[26]

Although Joy told herself that the three-dimensional material world was the only reality, she found this world boring, especially as it was portrayed in literature. Increasingly she was drawn to fantasy; George MacDonald's "Curdie" stories, *At the Back of the North Wind*, and *Phantastes* captivated her during childhood. As a teenager she was equally enthralled by the mystical poetry and novels of Lord Dunsany. Furthermore, as she recalled it, her "inner per-

sonality" became "deeply interested in Christ and didn't know it."
Joy remembered that

> as a Jew, I had been led to feel cold chills at the mention of
> his name. Is that strange? For a thousand years Jews have
> lived among people who interpreted Christ's will to mean
> floggings and burnings, "gentleman's agreements," and
> closed universities. If nominal Christians so confuse their
> Master's teaching, surely a poor Jew may be pardoned a little
> confusion. Nevertheless I read the Bible (for its literary beauty,
> of course!) and I quoted Jesus unconsciously in everything I
> did, from writing verse to fighting my parents.[27]

Joy's first published poem was entitled "Resurrection." She
described it in later years as "a sort of private argument with Jesus,
attempting to convince him (and myself) that he had never risen."
Almost incredibly and certainly unintentionally she wrote "Resurrection" at Easter and "never guessed why" until she was in her
thirties.[28]

"Resurrection" was not Joy's only poem to focus on Jesus of
Nazareth. Most of her early verses included the symbol of the
cross; Joy explained this to her atheist father and friends by saying
that the Christians' Messiah is "a very valuable literary convention."
Many years later she recalled that "Those verses were mainly the
desperate question: Is life really only a matter of satisfying one's
appetites, or is there more?"[29]

Outwardly Joy answered, "There is no more." But inwardly
she was haunted, haunted by a recurring dream: "I would walk
down a familiar street which suddenly grew unfamiliar and
opened onto a strange, golden, immeasurable plain, where far
away there rose the towers of Fairyland. If I remembered the way
carefully, the dream told me, I should be able to find it when I
woke up." She was told by those who embraced conventional

psychology that "such visions are merely 'wishful thinking.'" But Joy kept asking, "Why should all human beings be born with something like that, unless it exists?" This "Legend of the Way Out" is grounded in ancient mythology, "the door leading out of time and space into Somewhere Else." Joy was intrigued by Thomas Wolfe's description of the legend: "a stone, a leaf, an unfound door." She believed that we all cross that threshold in death, but for centuries writers of fantasy and mythology have maintained that "for a few lucky ones the door has swung open *before* death, letting them through, perhaps for the week of fairy time which is seven long years on earth; or at least granting them glimpses of the other side."[30]

C. S. Lewis, too, had been continually haunted by the vision from childhood on; he described it in *Pilgrim's Regress* as the Island. Soon after his conversion to Christianity, Lewis developed the idea as part of his argument in defense of Christianity. Joy could not yet accept his conclusions—the supernatural as fact was still beyond her grasp in the 1930s—but she found the notion delightful in fiction.[31]

While there would be no relief from the dream for some time, there were diversions. Joy attended P. S. 21 in Woodlawn for six grades, then finished Angelo Patri Junior High School on Fordham Road at age ten. Although she had had two six-month absences due to illness, Joy completed the program at Evander Childs High School at age fourteen—a prodigious achievement. She graduated in January 1930, but stayed on and took courses for the remainder of the year.[32]

In September 1930 Joy entered Hunter College in the Bronx. Part of the City University system, it had been established as a tuition-free women's college in 1870. When Joy enrolled in 1930, the institution had four buildings on an attractive thirty-seven-acre campus.[33] Joy continued to live at home in the Bronx with her parents; this kept her tied more closely to her parents, more than most college students, but she was only fifteen and hardly ready to go out on her own.

Although she still answered to her father, during the Hunter College years, Joy took her first steps toward liberation and maturation. Novelist Bel Kaufman, perhaps best known today for *Up the Down Staircase*, was Joy's closest friend at Hunter. Kaufman remembers her well. When Joy arrived at Hunter, she was slightly plump for her 5 foot 2 inch frame. Her piercing brown eyes, short dark hair, and beautiful complexion were appealing and distracted people from her poor taste in clothes. Like Bel Kaufman, Joy was an English major with a passion for writing short stories and poetry. Joy was recognized as being exceptionally bright, well read, and quite sophisticated intellectually—if a bit naïve and immature socially.[34]

While Joy loved her courses in English and French literature, she positively reveled in her work as associate editor of the Hunter College *Echo*, the in-house literary magazine, where she developed some editorial skills. *Echo* published some of her short stories and poems, as well as translations she had done of poems by others. Already proficient in German and Latin, she learned French in college, and taught herself Greek in her spare time at home. Although she was active in the English club and Sigma Tau Delta, the national English studies honorary society, the aspiring young writer made few friends besides Edith Miller, on the *Echo* staff, and Bel Kaufman.

Joy seldom dated. When she did go out, her escorts were older men seriously interested in literature. Joy found most college-aged men silly and boring, but this was probably the result of her shyness. If she decided to have a party at home—and she did so occasionally—she always turned to Bel as her mentor. What should I do? What should I serve? What will I say? For answers to these questions, she counted on Bel.[35]

In one area, Joy took strides well beyond Bel and the other students: Joy embarked on an affair with one of her professors, a man old enough to have a child her age. If Joy made him feel young, this Phi Beta Kappa with a doctorate from Columbia University made her feel important and sophisticated. No doubt part of his appeal was as a father figure she could love and trust. If she felt any guilt, it was not apparent; she unveiled the liaison to Bel and to her brother with an air of pride and accomplishment.[36]

Before Franklin D. Roosevelt had finished his first term as President, Joy Davidman had achieved some remarkable milestones. She had graduated from college before her twentieth birthday; she had lost her virginity to the man of her choice; she had savored the headiness of seeing her first poems and stories in print; and she had gained at least a modicum of independence from her parents. But exciting as these experiences were, they left her feeling still unsettled. Inside her there remained a vague sort of restlessness that would not go away, and there was an emptiness that no person or accomplishment could fill.

The feeling that there was something more than the material realm returned again and again. Joy even wrote a story, published in *Echo* in November 1934, entitled "Apostate," about a young Jewish woman named Chinya, living in a Russian village. Significantly, Chinya's father is mean and stingy. In the story, he is about to betroth his daughter to a small, weak man whom she dislikes because the fiancé would accept her with a small dowry. On the eve of the wedding, Chinya elopes with a strong and enticing Christian who will marry her if she will be baptized. Just before the baptism is performed, Chinya's father and brothers invade the ceremony and mercilessly beat the helpless apostate. Her Christian groom-to-be raises no hand in her defense, the pastor flees, and the Christian bystanders laugh as she is kicked and beaten by her own kin.

"Apostate" is a powerful story. It won the Bernard Cohen Short Story Prize at Hunter the year it was published. Perhaps this tale, set in nineteenth-century Russia, was no more than Joy's rendition of a story she heard from her mother about the Old World; on the other hand, it is tempting to see it as Joy herself wrestling with apostasy. It is possible that the budding writer had a need to tell her inner self that Chinya's choice is unworthy of an intelligent young Jewish woman, because apostasy would end in pain.

If "Apostate" helped her sort through conscious or unconscious temptations to flirt with Christianity, another story she published in *Echo*, entitled "Reveal the Titan," was certainly a therapeutic way of liberating herself from the pain of her dead-end love affair. "Reveal the Titan" is about a man who leaves a woman after an affair to pursue his obsession with music. Six years later he returns to his former lover and learns that she has had his child. Despite affection for her and a desire to assume his responsibility as a father, he cannot bring himself to allow marriage to compromise his total devotion to composition.

Whatever significance can be attached to these stories, Joy did not see apostasy or marriage as reasonable ways to fill her needs. Her immediate prescription for fulfillment was to put Hunter College and her lover behind her. She was looking ahead to new challenges.

Chapter 2

WANDERINGS (1934–1946)

"By God, I Am a Communist"

One afternoon in 1934, a few weeks before graduation, Joy glanced out of a classroom window at Hunter College just in time to see a young woman on the roof of an adjoining wing of the building; in a minute the poor wretch jumped to her death. Later Joy learned that the dead girl was a Depression-ravaged orphan who had been hungry for several days. Death was the only escape she saw from her predicament.

Joy couldn't forget this tragedy. Indeed, the girl's suicidal plunge was in her mind continually, and her anger grew increasingly at the insanity and callousness of a society that dumped potatoes in the ocean, burned wheat, and poured lime on oranges, while millions of people were unemployed, malnourished, and forced to stand in soup lines and sort through refuse in garbage cans for sustenance.[1]

Before the 1930s Joy had shared the assumptions held by most Americans. She believed that the capitalistic system was good, or at least neutral. Things were growing better in America; people were getting ahead. Few families that she encountered ended a

year worse off than they had been when it began. But the Great
Depression of the 1930s eventually changed those perceptions.
The Depression proved, to her mind, that the capitalistic system
had failed, the promise of American life was ending, and the idea
of progress was a sham. To be sure, the Davidman family was sur-
viving the Depression without trauma. Jen and Joe continued to
draw their paychecks from the public school system. The rent was
always paid; food was plentiful and nourishing, and there was even
money left over to save and to spend on college and vacations. But
increasingly, Joy looked beyond the perimeter of her own little
world and was troubled by what she saw.

In fall 1934 the young college graduate took a position teaching English at Walton High School. She also enrolled in the master's program in English literature at Columbia University.
Attending the university and teaching children in a comfortable
middle-class school allowed Joy to ignore some of the shocking
misery caused by the nation's economic collapse. Then Joy's old
thyroid problem returned; and she was forced to resign her teaching position, slow down work on her master's degree program,
resume the radium collar treatments, and rest.

In December 1935 Joy was awarded a master's degree in English literature. Typically, she had honors marks in her major, and
she took some advanced work in French literature as well. Still
recuperating from the bout with thyrotoxicosis, Joy wrote poetry
and looked forward to returning to teaching the next fall.[2]

The year 1936 was a difficult one for Joy Davidman. Howard
went off to the University of Virginia to complete his premed
undergraduate studies. This ended forever the closeness of two
siblings who had been confidants, shared scores of movies and
adventures, and stood together in league against parents and the
world.[3] To fill the empty hours Joy enrolled in some evening grad-

uate courses in the School of Education at the College of the City of New York. There she met Abraham Poneman, another graduate student and English teacher, and they dated sporadically for a year or so.[4]

Going to movies and taking walks with Abraham helped fill the void of Howard's absence for Joy, but this new relationship did nothing to soothe the trauma caused by Joy's new teaching position. In fall 1936 Joy was assigned to the English faculty at Roosevelt High School. Unlike Walton High School, where the students were economically well situated and thoroughly Americanized, Roosevelt's district was populated with students from the lower income classes, many of whom were relatively new immigrants. Joy remembered how difficult it was trying "to teach *Ivanhoe* to second-term Italian-Americans, who hardly knew English because it wasn't spoken at home."[5]

To make matters worse, Joy Davidman, Abraham Poneman, and all other new teachers were placed by the school system in a newly created category of "permanent substitutes." Even after passing the examinations required to become regular teachers, the faculty who entered the teaching system during the Depression were kept in this substitute category for years because the salaries for those positions ranged from $21 to $37 a week—considerably lower than the pay scale of tenured faculty. While this might have been a logical way for the school board to cut costs during the Depression, it was uniformly unpopular with new faculty.

Joy not only disliked the discriminatory salaries paid "permanent substitutes," she resented the additional chores such as floor-scrubbing, typing, and mimeographing that her category of teachers was required to perform.[6] These conditions, as well as the fact that she found no real satisfaction in teaching, led her to resign in summer of 1937. With the luxury of being able to live at home at her parents' expense she planned to devote herself to writing poetry and fiction, using her talents and energy for remaking an economic system that caused the orphaned to commit suicide and exploited teachers. Surely now she would find meaning and fulfillment in her life.

Initially, Joy devoted much time to writing. Her youthful ambition to be a writer—a dream nurtured by her writing achievements as an undergraduate at Hunter—was whetted by new publishing successes. In January 1936, *Poetry*, the prestigious "little magazine" edited by the venerable Harriet Monroe, brought out several of Joy's poems. In March 1937 four more of her pieces appeared in that important periodical.[7] Although Harriet Monroe died in fall 1936, Joy's association with the editor went back two years and opened important doors for the future. Joy had not only impressed Monroe with her skill as a poet, but had demonstrated a keen critical eye as well. Indeed, Monroe frequently employed Joy to read verse that was submitted to *Poetry* in 1935 and 1936.[8]

It was Monroe's encouragement that led Joy to an acquaintance with Stephen Vincent Benét, the celebrated novelist and poet. In late 1937 Joy submitted a collection of nearly fifty poems to Benét, who was at the time editor of the Younger Poet Series published by the Yale University Press. Competition for publication in this distinguished series was keen, and Benét was inundated with manuscripts. Yet he read every submission himself, maintaining that it was worth the effort if he came upon one good manuscript in fifty. As editor he was frequently denounced by poets who held higher opinions of their work than did Benét; nevertheless, he stood his ground, noting somewhat sadly that he could only publish one volume a year, thus leaving many good manuscripts orphaned. "What I keep looking for," he told one poet, "is the live nerve, the live person speaking."[9] Clearly, Joy Davidman was one of these inspired people. In November 1938 *Letter to a Comrade*, a collection of forty-five of Joy's poems, was published in Benét's

Yale series. Only half a dozen of these pieces had appeared in print before, and Benét enthusiastically endorsed Joy as a poet with "an intelligent, sensitive, and vivid mind," one who saw the world quite differently than did the writers of the 1920s. She saw, he wrote, "with accuracy and freshness," and her verse, both free and more traditional, contained "genuine power."[10]

Most of the critics were kind to *Letter to a Comrade*. Ruth Lechlitner in *Books* said, "Joy Davidman's poems are important. . . . They show genuine ability as they refreshingly present to us what a generation that did not know war thinks about our times." Dorothy Ulrich in *The New York Times* maintained that "Miss Davidman's greatest facility is in disciplined verse—occasionally marred by false rhymes—but it may be that she promises most in the freer forms which, harsh and strained though they sometimes seem, are effectively harmonized with the material." This criticism notwithstanding, Ulrich argued that the book "is distinguished, on the whole, for its plasticity of technique, clarity of image, affirmative strength and flexibility of thought." Oscar Williams, writing for *Poetry*, noted that while "there is a veritable army of young poets each year trying to make the grade of the Yale Series of Younger Poets, Joy Davidman has deservedly won out for 1938. Her first book is a big one—more than 80 pages heavily packed with rhymed and unrhymed verse and a great deal of promise." He did, however, wish she had "condensed" the volume. If she had done so "we might have had a remarkable first volume."[11]

The verse in *Letter to a Comrade* tells us much about Joy in the late 1930s. "Prayer Against Indifference" shows her disdain for social apathy:

> When wars and ruined men shall cease
> To vex my body's house of peace,
> And bloody children lying dead

Let me lie softly in my bed
To nurse a whole and sacred skin,
Break roof and let the bomb come in.

She was a thoroughly urban woman, and this is strikingly revealed in "Twentieth-Century Americanism":

Come now all Americans
kiss and accept your city, the harsh mother,
New York, the clamor, the sweat, the heart of brown
land,
the gold heart and the stone heart, the best of
American blood,
the cat stretching out before a borrowed fire
beside the steam heat, in apartment houses.

. . . This is New York,
our city; a kind place to live in; beautiful; our city
envied by the world and by the young in lonely places.
We have the bright-lights, the bridges, the Yankee
Stadium
and if we are not contented then we should be
and if we are discontented we do not know it,
and anyhow it always has been this way.

Joy's growing radical tendencies neither permeated nor overwhelmed the book, but they were present in the title and in such poems as "Apology for Liberals" and "End of a Revolutionary," and echoed in lines like "Assault the door, break down the door, break open the door" in "Spartacus 1938."

She celebrated an incipient feminism in "This Woman":

Now do not put a ribbon in your hair;
Abjure the spangled insult of design,

The filigree sterility, nor twine
A flower with your strength, go bare, go bare.

The wounds of her undergraduate affair were clearly slow to heal. She laid them open in "An Absolution":

Let the red image of my agony
Move you no more than to a cool regret
For inconsiderable sorrow.

And in "Jewess to Aryan," she exuded pain:

. . . you coward to eat the body out and leave . . .
I have resented you; a parasite worm drinking the
        female . . .
You needed me to divert your mind. . . .

Significantly, Joy's writing reflected her continuing fascination with Christianity, especially with Jesus, the Crucifixion, and the Resurrection. A poem entitled "And Pilate Said" is quite revealing, as is another one suggestively titled "Againrising," which contains much symbolism:

The noonday struck
a note of pride;
spread on the clock
I was crucified. . . .

The sound of seven
filled me with bells;
I left great heaven
for little hells. . . . [12]

Letter to a Comrade sold quite well for poetry. Stephen Vincent Benét hoped that "Miss Davidman's book will reach a rather larger audience than that generally reserved for first books of verse."[13] It did. The first printing sold out immediately, and a second printing was ordered in spring 1939. Nearly half a century later the book is still in print. Such a happy fate is experienced by few modern poets.

Stephen Vincent Benét, who had by this time won the Pulitzer Prize for his epic poem, *John Brown's Body*, was an immense help and inspiration to Joy. He not only gave her valuable criticism and assisted her in publishing her first book, but also introduced her to Carl Brandt. A New York literary agent, Brandt took Joy on as one of his company's select group of authors. Brandt assigned Joy's work to Bernice Baumgarten, one of his company's agents. Thanks to Benét, in the late 1930s Joy Davidman began a relationship with Brandt & Brandt that was to last her lifetime.[14]

Benét also acquainted Joy with the MacDowell Colony at Peterborough, New Hampshire. Benét had visited this colony for both established artists and younger people of talent in literature and the fine arts, and he encouraged Joy to go there. She did so in the summer of 1938, and again in 1940, 1941, and 1942. During the latter summer Laura Benét, Stephen's sister, was there, too.

The MacDowell Colony was extremely important to Joy, because it symbolized the cementing of her new identity as a writer. Located in southern New Hampshire at the edge of Peterborough, then a town of twenty-five hundred people, MacDowell embraced over six hundred acres. Much of the landscape, lying in the valley where the Nubanusit and Contoocook Rivers meet, was covered in fir and birch, and Grand Monadnock Mountain graced the western horizon. Edward MacDowell, the composer, and his wife, Marian, a noted pianist, purchased the old farm property in 1898 as a retreat for rest and composition. In 1907, Edward and Marian decided to build more studios on this land so that other creative people—artists and writers as well as musicians—could come and find solitude for their work. Although Edward died in 1908, while still in his forties, Marian carried on the task of building the colony with marked success. By the time Joy arrived thirty-three buildings dotted the land. Twenty-three artists' cottages or studios stood within walking distance of residence halls, a library, an assembly hall, and dining room. Several other structures, including "Log Cabin," where Edward had worked, and "Hillcrest," the home of Marian and the same house where she and Edward spent their summers beginning in 1898, completed the colony.

Writers and artists applied to the colony for periods of one to three months. Talent was the only criterion for selection. The people chosen paid their own expenses if they could; fees for those unable to support themselves were underwritten by a private corporation originally endowed by such notables as theologian and author Henry Van Dyke, industrialist Andrew Carnegie, financier J. P. Morgan, and former President Grover Cleveland.

Among those who had been to MacDowell before Joy were Willa Cather, Edward Arlington Robinson, Sara Teasdale, and Louis Untermeyer. Like them and all the others who visited MacDowell, Joy lived in a residence hall and ate breakfast and dinner with the other colonists in the common dining room. During the day the artists spent their time in private studio cottages, where they were not subject to interruptions. Lunch was left in baskets on the door step, and only emergency messages or phone calls were delivered during working hours. Marian MacDowell, who actively managed the colony until her death in 1956, saw to it that the artists who received her hospitality were free to work in a sanctuary of quiet and natural beauty.[15]

Joy made good use of the MacDowell Colony. With *Letter to a Comrade* already safely in press at Yale, she spent the summer of 1938 finishing a novel entitled *Anya*, started over a year before.

Dedicated "to my mother, who told me the story of Anya," *Anya* was published in July 1940 by Macmillan.

Anya tells the story of a late nineteenth-century Jewish woman in a small Ukrainian village. Howard Davidman recalled that while most of the names were changed, the characters and events of *Anya* were based upon real people and episodes remembered by their mother from childhood. Joy even kept the name of Tulchin, the Ukrainian village from which her mother emigrated, in the novel. In fact, the story was so graphic and truthful to Jen's memories that she viewed the publication of *Anya* with trepidation and mixed feelings. She was at once immensely proud of her daughter's accomplishment and fearful that the characters might be recognized.[16]

Nearly three hundred pages long, the novel is a well-written and fast-moving story of Anya's life and loves from adolescence to middle age. The book is filled with humor, suspense, and pathos. A tale of maturation, it carries Anya through one premarital sexual encounter, marriage, several pregnancies, and three extramarital love affairs before she comes to terms with herself, settles down, and promises her husband she will never leave him again.

While the protagonist and many episodes came from Joy's mother's memory, the themes and their development are vintage Joy Davidman. Anya is, foremost, a liberated woman. No culture can contain her or dictate to her; at one point, Anya says, "No man shall have power over me." Joy's unabashed sensuality comes through in nearly every chapter. Anya is not a wanton woman, as most of the inhabitants of Tulchin believe. Rather she is so emotionally, physically, and mentally alive that she is incapable—given the structure of her culture—of containing herself as she seeks meaning, fulfillment, and freedom. As the dust jacket on the first printing put it, "Like its heroine, this novel is glowing, sensuous, alive. It is written in a vein suggesting D. H. Lawrence, with poetic artistry and with all five senses awake to the warmth, color, and feel of things."[17]

There is a hint of naturalism in the novel. For example, when Anya is taken sexually—she is not raped, but she does not really give herself—by a young man named Yankov, Joy writes:

> She had just time to feel strangely elated because he was so strong, and to understand that this, a necessary, an inevitable, a preordained thing, could not be stopped, before her hatred ebbed and melted away leaving only the loving flesh.[18]

In *Anya* outside forces do not overwhelm people as they do in the fiction of Emile Zola or Frank Norris; and Anya is certainly not victimized like Stephen Crane's Maggie. Anya is, within certain boundaries, quite free. Obviously Joy, now in her early twenties, was sorting out her beliefs about free will.

Reminiscent of the work of D. H. Lawrence, *Anya* brings to mind the fiction of Isaac Bashevis Singer. Like the great Polish-born Nobel Laureate, Joy produced a piece of literature that serves as a bridge between this century and an obliterated past. In *Anya* the reader glimpses the nineteenth-century shtetl—complete with sharp details of dress, customs, food, houses, furnishings, and Yiddish expressions. Because Joy preaches more, she is harder on the law than is Singer. But even when she does attack tradition, it is with a good sense of humor. When one of her characters drives off a sow that is trying to devour a little boy, she hits the creature "with a stick of firewood in her left hand and a copper pan in her right." While the child is saved, it is "too bad about the copper pan, which had muck all over its bright shiny tinned inside and was probably ceremonially unclean too because of having hit a pig."[19]

The critics were even more laudatory toward *Anya* then they had been to *Letter to a Comrade*. When the reviews appeared in summer 1940, they were uniformly favorable. Alfred Kazin missed the point a bit by calling it a comedy, but he was correct in saying that it was written without "dross and tears," and that it was "fresh." In *The New York Times* John Cournos celebrated *Anya* by saying "this is a powerful, well-written novel," and "Anya is real and thoroughly alive." N. L. Rothman, who reviewed it for the *Saturday Review of Literature* dignified the author by observing that "whatever the term 'first novel' implies, 'Anya' is free of it. It is the full-blown, beautifully written work of a deep artistic intelligence." Rothman went on to point out that "Miss Davidman has a natural flair for fresh and immediate seeing, and a sure knowledge of the swells and starts of emotion. Better, she can write what she sees and knows."[20]

Anya is a book about a young woman full of life, awake to the world around her, never satisfied until she touches and experiences more and then more, but it is also a book about Joy Davidman. She had found success in publishing poetry and fiction. By summer 1938, her works had appeared in *Poetry*; *Letter to a Comrade* was at press, and the manuscript of *Anya* had been finished and accepted by Macmillan. She had discovered the MacDowell Colony and fallen in love with the world of writers and other creative people. Nevertheless, like Anya, Joy was not satisfied. There had to be more.

Her productivity at the typewriter notwithstanding, Joy's enthusiasm for life, and her inner drive to find her own niche—the place where she fit and could find meaning and peace—fired a dynamo that knew no rest. Part of her restlessness came from the suicide she had witnessed three years previously. It continued to haunt her conscience. No amount of writing, no letters of acceptance from publishers, no elation engendered by chats with other writers allowed her to ignore the abject poverty left in the wake of the Depression. In fact, Joy's growing disdain for the values, institutions, and political philosophy that led to economic collapse and then excused the turning of deaf ears to the cries of the impoverished, eventually transformed her into a radical with missionarylike zeal.

At MacDowell, when Joy felt tense and frustrated, she went swimming or hiking. One day, her nerves screaming, she went for a long walk to contemplate the wretchedness in the world. Sorting through various panaceas in her mind, it occurred to her, "If I keep on thinking like this I'll be a Communist." She stopped abruptly on the pathway, took an honest look at herself, and somewhat surprisedly exclaimed, "By God, I am a Communist."[21]

Many young Americans, especially artists and intellectuals, jumped on the Communist bandwagon prior to World War II. Numerous college friends of Joy's were already in the Party, so the notion of joining was hardly unique. The stated goals of the Party—full employment, equality of opportunity, abolition of discrimination toward blacks, women, Jews, and other minorities, and destruction of fascism—were downright alluring to sensitive people during the 1930s.[22]

"Maybe no rational person would worry about the rest of the world; I found myself worrying, all the same. And I wanted to *do* something, so I joined the Communist Party," said Joy.[23] The young writer contemplated the move toward membership for several months before she took it. To be sure, Joy knew her own mind, and seldom let convention stand in the way of her will. But she was still living at home and enjoying the free room and board that enabled her to pursue her writing habit. And while she rather enjoyed shocking people, particularly her parents, she knew that joining the Communist Party would cause a thunderous explosion at home. Her Fabian socialist father was not only a gradualist who deplored the Communist Party's commitment to revolution, he was a public school administrator who disliked anything that made enemies or attracted unfavorable attention to himself or his family. Although he professed socialism, he always remained firmly within the respectability of the Democratic Party's left wing.

By late 1938 Joy could no longer contain her enthusiasm. Knowing she was a Communist at heart was not enough; one evening, she visited a college classmate who was in the Party, and expressed her desire to become a member. Her friend from Hunter was apparently rather skeptical. Instead of welcoming Joy with open arms, she sent her home with some literature and a curt "Read the literature. Then we'll talk some more."[24]

"My motives were a mixed lot," Joy recalled. "Youthful rebelliousness, youthful vanity, youthful contempt of the 'stupid people' who seemed to be running society, all these played a part." The world needed to be overhauled and who was better to do it than Joy Davidman, the brilliant young writer? Joy remembered that

> art had something to do with my decision, for those were the years in which great films and books and music were coming out of the Soviet Union. The war in Spain had much to do with it. Most of all, however, I think I was moved by the same unseen power that had directed my reading and dreaming—I became a Communist because, later on, I was going to become a Christian.[25]

Whatever the motives, an inherent commitment to Party orthodoxy was not the impetus. When Joy spoke to her Party-member friend, she revealed something of her concern for the world's downtrodden as she reiterated her desire to become a card-carrying affiliate. The sagacious friend brought Joy up short with a caustic, "Wait a minute. You mean you want to join for the sake of *other people?*" "Then and there I told my first lie for the Party. Her tone warned me that I was in danger of rejection." Joy promptly retorted, "To hell with other people. I want to join the Communists for my own sake, because I know I can't have a decent future without Socialism!" Her friend breathed a relieved sigh and smiled. And Joy knew that her "Marxist education, the process of getting rid of [her] 'bourgeois values,' had begun."[26]

Those who saw the American Communist Party of the 1930s as a real threat to democracy, effectively redirecting good citizens into subversive activities, would have slept easier had they witnessed Joy's "initiation." On three different occasions she joined the Party. Her first two tries were aborted by sloppy record keeping. One evening at a downtown West Side branch, she and half a dozen others took the oath to Karl Marx and the working class, but no card was forthcoming. She joined again at a large rally in Madison Square Garden, but no formal membership credentials followed the loyalty-oath ceremony. Finally, on a valiant third attempt, she went to a meeting on lower Fifth Avenue with a date. The young man brought her luck. This time she succeeded in being sworn in, and the leadership gave her a card and a dues book. "If I succeed in making only one thing clear," she told a reporter three years after she left the Party, "I hope it will be to disabuse the public of the notion that the ordinary American Communist is an angelic superman, or a diabolic superman. In fact, he is plain Joe Doakes. Communists aren't much more careless or ignorant than other people, they're just prouder of it!"[27]

Like many members, Joy took on a Party name. "Nell Tulchin" was her choice, Tulchin being on Joy's mind at this time because she had just wrapped up *Anya* and sent it off to her agent at Brandt & Brandt. But within a year Joy dropped the alias and "thereafter sailed under her own colors."[28]

Joe and Jen Davidman ranted and raved about their daughter's latest eccentricity, but did little besides make noise. They would hardly have thrown her out on the street in any case, but their attention was drawn away from the Communist Party because of the flood of good fortune that came Joy's way in winter 1938–39. *Letter to a Comrade* made its debut in November at two dollars a copy, and it soon won the Loines Memorial Fund award given by the National Institute of Arts and Letters. The award brought with it a prize of one thousand dollars.[29] Joy reveled in the good fortune of the honor, the usefulness of the stipend, and the added glory that came because she was named co-recipient with Robert Frost. That she was traveling in company with the august New England poet was not lost on Joe and Jen. All of Joy's sins were forgiven— for the time being.

As soon as Joy received her card, she threw herself into the work of the Communist Party. If she was going to change the world, then she had to get on with it. Immediately her talents were put to use by the Party. "With my few scraps of knowledge, I was accepted almost at once as a journalist and critic on the Party's semiofficial magazine *New Masses*."[30] That the magazine could not pay her at the outset was of no importance; Joy was housed, fed, and clothed at home, and her writing was going well and bringing in some money, too. On staff at *New Masses* Joy remembered

> I began to learn. I learned that "love of the people" turned into quite specific hatred of the people's enemies, and that the enemies of the people were all those of every class and opinion who happened to disagree with the Party. Hatred, to us, was a virtue, and, much as we hated Fascism, we hated even more bitterly the anti-Fascist liberals who were our rivals for the support of labor.[31]

The new convert was exuberant—even arrogant—in her new faith and position at *New Masses*. She thoroughly enjoyed her role as resident sage, especially her responsibility as poetry critic.

Art was now purposeful, and that purpose was sharply political. Evaluating manuscripts was heady duty, too. She enjoyed the power to accept or reject authors' submissions immensely, and she delighted in telling others about her seat of authority. Referring to Oscar Williams, who in an otherwise kind review made an unfavorable criticism of *Letter to a Comrade*, she boasted, "I had just rejected his awful masterpieces at the *New Masses*, but was too kind to tell him so."[32]

Joy particularly liked jolting people when she could, or at least rattling them with her extremist views. In a letter to poet Kenneth Porter, written soon after joining the *New Masses* staff, she ostentatiously let him know that she had lectured to the Poetry Society the previous evening. It must have been a delightful gathering for those in attendance because, she caustically noted, "Good God, what an assemblage of pathetic hangers-on of the arts. I mentioned politics and was nervously shushed." This, she decided, reminded her "of Shaw's criticism of polite conversation, that it excluded the only two topics worth discussing: religion and politics." With customary confidence that her angle of vision was the only valid one, she raised a rhetorical question to Porter: "How the blazes do people expect to write poetry in a vacuum? I told 'em so, but I imagine each listener mentally excepted himself from my accusations."[33]

On another occasion Joy blasted one of Porter's poems in a haughty manner. When he protested, she apologized—something she seldom did during her Communist years. Her recantation is important because it underscores her philosophy in 1939:

I was rather hasty in calling "the Lord's Supper" silly, I'm afraid. Looking at it now, I see it was the whole sacramental idea which annoyed me; I'm inclined by nature to call anything sacramental sentimental, being an iron materialist.[34]

The iron materialist was no sooner settled into her post at *New Masses* than another accolade came her way. During late 1938 Metro-Goldwyn-Mayer experimented with a young scriptwriter's program. Hoping to identify some fresh talent, M-G-M brought several young writers of promise to Hollywood and paid them fifty dollars a week for six months. The California-based company wrote to the heads of English departments at several Eastern colleges to collect names and recommendations. When Dr. Blanche Colton Williams at Hunter College was contacted, she put Joy's name on the list. The publication of the award-winning *Letter to a Comrade* and the acceptance of *Anya* gave Joy the clout she needed. In April 1939 she was selected.[35]

In a few weeks Joy Davidman invaded Hollywood. Canceling her plans to return to the MacDowell Colony that summer, she reveled for a time in the payment of her largest regular income to date, as well as the escape from her parents' watchful eyes. Flush with publishing success, she no doubt had lofty hopes for her future as a scriptwriter. But Hollywood markedly disappointed Joy, both personally and professionally. She had a brief affair with a Hollywood man that left her unfulfilled, if not guilt ridden or heartbroken.[36]

Without question, Joy was a talented writer; she had proved that with her verse and fiction. But no one at M-G-M liked her scriptwriting. She wrote at least four scripts—not one of which was translated onto film. Because Joy's ego was so inflated at the time, she was unable to take this failure in stride. Instead, she behaved like her father. He never failed or allowed failure; when he did fail, he blamed it on his partner. Joy had learned this technique well. When she saw the handwriting on the wall at the studio, she began cutting up and pretending she saw the entire industry as a joke. She spent her evenings at Communist Party meetings, made a show of coddling the M-G-M lion, and wrote a tongue-in-cheek script that infuriated the middle brass, and then acted as if she didn't care. After all, she rationalized, one couldn't do serious work with buffoons who employed and listened to sons and daughters unable to make the grade in good Eastern colleges.[37]

By autumn 1939 Joy retreated from Hollywood for good. Back in New York she boasted that she was delighted to be away from the visionless oafs with neither talent nor taste for art. It was convenient, too, that Stephen Vincent Benét had also been disenchanted with Hollywood, the film industry, and its managers. However, there was an important difference between their experiences. Benét earned a large fee for writing the screenplay for D. W. Griffith's *Abraham Lincoln*. Also, Benét's script had been accepted, and he left Hollywood by choice.[38]

The activities of the Communist Party in New York City, Joy now maintained, were her true calling. Picking up where she had left off, Joy immersed herself once again in work at *New Masses* and another book of poetry. This time there was a fervency— almost an urgency—that hadn't been apparent before the Hollywood adventure. She seemed desperate to prove to herself and those around her that only the Party and its purposes held any meaning.

Joy took to closing her letters with "comradely" or "dosvedanye [sic] tovarishch" and she began to measure friendship by judging lines of loyalty to the Soviet Union. One of her best friends in high school, the novelist Nina Schneider, remembered that she had kept in touch with Joy through "her Hollywood stint . . . but we lost each other to our differences over Communism. She was ardent. I was suspicious." The death blow to the relationship came when Nina refused, despite Joy's insistence, to "abandon friends who had 'turned'" or deserted the Party over the Hitler-Stalin nonaggression pact and their joint venture to invade and partition Poland.[39]

Joy not only made party-line loyalty the acid test of friendship; she now began to write with evangelistic fervor. *Anya* had no political message whatsoever, and *Letter to a Comrade* had only a title and few poems out of forty-five that were worthy of the cause. But after her Hollywood debacle Joy tried to use her talents as an editor, writer, and critic solely for the revolution. She became a member of the League of American Writers. Formed in the 1930s, the League was a Popular Front organization that stood on this platform:

> to fight against imperialist war and fascism, defend the
> Soviet Union against capitalist aggression; for the develop-
> ment and strengthening of the revolutionary labor move-
> ment; against white chauvinism (against all forms of Negro
> discrimination or persecution) and against persecution of
> minority groups and of the foreign-born; solidarity with
> Colonial people in their struggles for freedom; against the
> influence of bourgeois ideas in American liberalism; against
> the imprisonment of revolutionary writers and artists, as
> well as other class-war prisoners throughout the world.[40]

As historians of this movement have noted, "the document was characteristic of the new, ecumenical, moderated communism," in that "it retained the revolutionary vocabulary of class struggle while studiously avoiding any mention of the revolutionary goals of international communism (e.g., the overthrow of the bour-geois capitalist state)." The aim was to attract young writers in this way—especially blacks or members of the working class—and get them to use their writing skills for these ideals.[41]

As a member of the League of American Writers, Joy per-suaded the organization to sponsor a book of anti-imperialist war poetry. She served as editor. Ultimately published in 1943 by Dial Press as *War Poems of the United Nations*, the anthology included three hundred selections from 150 poets representing twenty countries. Joy's foreword to the volume sums up the book's purpose, content, and tone:

> To attempt a definitive collection of war poetry at this time would, of course, be grotesque. Much of the poetry of this war has yet to be written, some of it no doubt in retrospect ten years from now; much more is being written at this moment; of what has already been produced, much is inaccessible to American editors. Poems are an integral part of the underground movements in the occupied countries of Europe, but few of them have reached us. Nevertheless the war has already stimulated poets everywhere so much that an anthology like this one can provide a fair sample of the poetry of the anti-Fascist struggle.
>
> We have included in our definition of the war every conflict that has taken place since Hitler's first rise to power; the ten-year-long fight of China, the tragic battle of Republican Spain against Fascism, and the lonely struggles of German and Austrian anti-Fascists are as much part of the great crisis of our time as what is happening today in Africa. Thus we have been able to include the magnificent fighting poems of German and Spanish refugees, as well as poetry from many Latin American countries not actually at war. We have unfortunately been unable, in the time at our disposal, to procure poems from Jugoslavia, Greece, Belgium, and Holland. Our French section consists almost entirely of poems printed under Vichy, and gains a peculiar interest through the ingenuity with which its authors express anti-Fascist sentiment in veiled language. The section from the British Empire has been deliberately limited by us in order to exclude certain defeatist and

appeaser elements which are fortunately losing their quon-
dam influence on renascent British poetry.

In the section devoted to the United States, we have
concentrated on the work of new poets developed by the
war, some of whom are actually in the armed forces;
although most of the great names of American poetry are
also represented. The Soviet Russian section is unique in
being itself a small anthology of the war poems of many
different Soviet Republics, including Central Asian peoples
whose very names are little known here.

Franklin Folsom, who served as executive secretary of the
League between 1937 and 1942, knew Joy while she was editing
War Poems. She was, according to Folsom, "a driving person who
wanted to get the maximum attention for, and maximum income
from, this collection of verse."[42] The anthology was not a best-
seller; art as a weapon seldom is. And this particular volume, with
so many different poets contributing, was markedly uneven in
quality. Many of the poems had to be translated, often with devastating results to the power of the verse. Joy did many of the
translations herself, but the acknowledgments show that she
employed a stable full of translators to help her with the task.

Featured in *War Poems* were pieces originally published in
Poetry, New Masses, The Nation, The New Republic, The New Yorker,
and *Saturday Review*. Some of the contributors were such highly
respected and well-established literary figures as Carl Sandburg,
three of the Benéts (Laura, William Rose, and Stephen Vincent),
Boris Pasternak, and Langston Hughes. But others were
deservedly unknown poets who happened to be Joy's friends and
fellow travelers in Party circles. "Last Kilometer" for example, was
contributed by William Lindsay Gresham, her future husband. He
was dating Joy when the selections were made, and even he knew

he was not a poet. Two poets and their verse were the creations of Joy herself. She was unable to find any English poetry that served her purpose. Feeling certain such writing should exist even if she could not find it, the imaginative editor invented Megan Coombes-Dawson and Hayden Weir. To give Weir a stamp of glamorous authenticity, he was described as a heroic soldier who died in battle early in World War II.[43]

The League of American Writers collapsed in 1942, leaving Joy with the full responsibility for meeting "the terms of a formidable Dial Press contract," which called for a lengthy manuscript with extensive editorial work.[44] The obligation was fulfilled because Joy was an ultradependable person; Joe had brought her up to do things, do them well, and do them on time. Efficiency was a family trait that was so much a part of the Davidman parents and children that it seemed to be genetic.

Despite the large demands of this book, Joy found time to do other things for her new cause. She edited the poems of Alexander Bergman, a pathetic Party member who died of tuberculosis in 1941. Three days before this lonely man passed away, Joy visited him in New York's Montefiore Hospital, read some of his poems, and promised to get them into print and out to the public. True to her word, Joy arranged for Ackerman Press to bring out Bergman's work the following year in a volume entitled *They Looked Like Men*. Joy edited this little book, and she had several of the dead man's pieces published in *War Poems* and *New Masses*.[45]

Beyond editing two volumes of verse, Joy also organized numerous symposiums for the League of American Writers, including one that featured W. H. Auden and Christopher Isherwood. She oversaw the events, working hard to recruit young writers, among them Kenneth Porter, to come and join the fun.[46] Her motives, of course, were mixed. While she enjoyed the contact with other writers, conversions were what she sought. As one relative by marriage recalled, "She worked very hard to convert her good friends . . . to communism."[47]

Joy sought converts outside her circle of friends, too. She taught a night class of poetry for a communist front organization, where she was accurately billed as a published poet and winner of the Yale Younger Poets Series Award. Dressed in sweaters and tweed skirts, she made a vivid impression on her students. Jerome Hoffman, who was eighteen at the time, took one of her poetry-writing classes in an old building owned by the American Bible Society on New York City's Astor Place. It was 1942, and Hoffman was a college student who was getting ready for war and marriage, and trying to write poetry, too. He remembered Joy's course this way:

> The class turned out to be two young men (very young—
> eighteen each) and half a dozen older (forty? fifty?) people
> striving to express themselves in what may or may not have
> been poetry. The format was simple. We would each write
> one or more poems during the interval between classes,
> bring them into class, then read them aloud—usually—
> and Joy would criticize our efforts. She was very kind to the
> older people, but relatively merciless to the youngster [his
> friend] and me.[48]

Hoffman didn't get much out of the class because Joy seemed to show little genuine interest in the students and their work. Instead, her interest was in herself and in attacking what she didn't like. "Joy was extremely opinionated," he recalled. Before long, the class had dwindled to Joy, Hoffman, and his eighteen-year-old friend. The trio began to meet in a nearby tavern "for a beer (none of us could afford more than two, even at ten cents a large glass) and none of us were drinkers. To Hoffman, Joy:

was unattractive physically, not particularly ugly or interesting, but rather dumpy and though obviously female, rather
unfeminine. Her manner, and mannerisms, were almost a
stereotype of the 1930s radical. She was aggressive, impatient and intolerant. (So were we.) However, Joy was not an
anarchic radical. She had a system which she professed
complete belief and confidence in and tried to convert us. It
was the standard Communist Party line of the early 1940s,
with no original thought, variations, or input by Joy. I had
read the book of poetry which she had published [*Letter to
a Comrade*] and had listened to her in class and during our
beer discussions. I had not argued with her, but thought she
was an individualist in her political philosophy. That was
not the case. Her philosophy was rigid and admitted no
thought of God, of religion, of anything outside of dialec-
tic materialism. She was a New York Jewish girl (I am Jewish) who had rebelled against all religion and any
manifestation of religion.[49]

Joy continued to rebel against all religion, espousing the Party
line and seeking more recruits to help her remake the world. In
addition to all the hours she devoted to editing books, teaching
classes, and writing, she spent time on additional assignments at
New Masses, becoming a full-time employee in 1941 and even com-
manding a small salary of twenty-five dollars a week. Joy's duties
at *New Masses* were manifold, the major tasks being writing
reviews of books and movies and serving as poetry editor.

Although Joy was earning some money and doing what she
ardently maintained was meaningful work, she was unsettled and
angry. Somewhere deep down inside there was a haunting sore-
ness. This was evident in some of her behavior. On one occasion,

for example, when she and several friends were dining out and they saw a black person denied entry to the restaurant, Joy stood up and yelled, "What the hell are we waiting for!" With this battle cry she led the party out without finishing its meal—and, of course, without paying. Another outburst occurred when Joy asked a woman in front of her at a movie theater to remove her large hat. The woman ignored the request, and Joy ripped the hat from her head, hurling it to the front of the theater. The horrified woman fled, leaving her popcorn and hat behind.[50]

Her inner hurt was likewise evident in the vituperative quality of much of the work Joy turned out at *New Masses*. Her need to elevate herself by attacking others was nowhere clearer than in her reviews of films. Joy called *Andy Hardy's Private Secretary* "ridiculous," and labeled the acting of Gary Cooper and Barbara Stanwyck in *Meet John Doe* "utterly miserable" and "a soggy stain on the film," respectively.[51] She berated *The Bugle Sounds* as the worst of war films: "We used to like this when we were six, but not when we were seven."[52] Sometimes her attacks on Hollywood were accompanied by reports on her own activities. After one scathing denunciation she noted that "if these comments seem unduly severe, remember that this reviewer has just returned from a vacation in the pure air of New Hampshire to plunge back into films. And now she needs New Hampshire again."[53]

To write off Joy's sometimes mean-spirited comments as sour grapes would be simplistic. On occasion she could be generous toward America's movie industry, even at her own expense. In an April 1941 review of *Rage in Heaven* she was extremely kind to the overall effect of the writing, casting, and theme. Furthermore, she confessed that "this writer had a crack at writing it, too, in her Metro-Goldwyn-Mayer days, and it is with great magnanimity that she admits the film is much better than she or James Hilton left it."

Most likely her anger stemmed from being pressured to judge a book or a film "not on its artistic merit, but on its Marxist orthodoxy, or even on whether its author was a liberal contributor to the Party's needy treasury."[54] This made her feel increasingly dishonest. But she was in deep water at this point, and she had difficulty facing her growing disillusionment. To admit that the Communist Party was wrong, especially after her exibitionist-style display of commitment, would have been a second defeat or mistake too soon after Hollywood, and Joseph Davidman's daughter couldn't do that yet.

After accepting a salaried appointment at *New Masses* she espoused the Party line with the enthusiasm of a true believer. In a May 27, 1941, review of the Soviet Russian film, *Volga-Volga*, she exclaimed, "Do the Soviets *have* to come out on top in everything? They already have the best diplomats, the best kindergartens, the best economic system, the best life—but is that enough for them? No; they go and get the best musical comedies too. I turn green. I gnash my teeth with envy. It isn't fair. [*Volga-Volga*] has a laugh about every ten seconds, and good laughs too." In the same vein she reviewed a Soviet documentary, *Soviet Frontiers on the Danube*, which showed Red Army soldiers in Bessarabia: "This reviewer," Joy reminded her readers, "does not, ordinarily, label films 'must'; but *Soviet Frontiers on the Danube* is a 'must' picture."[55]

Gradually, however, Joy's intellectual and artistic integrity began to creep into her reviews. Although she continued to praise the films of the Soviets, she didn't do so convincingly. Commenting on *The Girl from Leningrad*, for example, she prefaced it by saying that "we are all weary of the theme of the nurse and the wounded soldier, where the two lovers end up together in the hospital." But in the Soviet rendition, she assures prospective moviegoers, it is not "trite." With the same lack of persuasion, she noted that "there is a particularly brilliant moment in which the city-bred nurses milk their first cow—old stuff, but still good."[56]

Now and then she broke down and celebrated Hollywood productions, especially if they starred Peter Lorre, Bette Davis, James Cagney, Edward G. Robinson, John Garfield, Ida Lupino, Clark Gable, or Humphrey Bogart; she also applauded films if their messages were totally apolitical, particularly detective mysteries or screwball comedies.[57] But Joy was criticized by the *New Masses* editors for these lapses into "bourgeois values," and she was pressured into complimenting actors she didn't admire because of their involvement in the Screen Actors Guild.[58]

Joy held onto her image as a faithful Communist long after she had drifted away in her mind and heart because she had little else to hold onto. Among the wedges separating her from orthodoxy were the pressures to write dishonest reviews and what she saw as the Party members' incredibly inconsistent view of the law. "I couldn't see why Communists should appeal to the law to protect them when they felt no obligation to live according to the law."[59] Likewise, Joy was bothered by an assignment involving a book review in early 1943. The Book-of-the-Month Club was about to circulate a sharply anti-Communist Party novel. Because of her hatchet jobs on movies, Joy was assigned the task of infiltrating the BOMC offices to get a story on the author, the book, and the promotional campaign. Joy was to pose as one inclined to do a friendly article, when in reality her assignment was to deprecate the book and everyone involved. But stricken by conscience at the last moment, and fearful for the future of the young woman who had arranged for Joy to get inside at BOMC, the *New Masses* associate editor (Joy's title until November 1943) dropped for a moment her image as a tough radical. After confessing her intention to write a feature "of the nasty, *New Yorkerish* sort," she was respectfully but firmly denied any more cooperation.[60]

As much as anything, Joy's marriage to William Lindsay Gresham in August 1942 brought on her rupture with the Communist Party. Although her ties with the radicals did not end until 1946, her relationship with them grew weaker and weaker with each passing year. Joy met Bill Gresham, a freelance writer and Spanish War veteran, at a Communist Party function. Soon after their wedding, Joy said, "We made a startling discovery: marriage had ended, overnight, all our lingering interest in going to Party social gatherings! I realized then a hitherto unsuspected attraction for the young which the Communist Party shares with the church social—it is a great matchmaker."[61]

With the hindsight of several years, Joy analyzed her drift from Communism in this way:

> My husband had lost his enthusiasm for Communist
> speeches in Spain. What war did for him childbirth did for
> me. My little son was a real thing and so was my obligation
> to him; by comparison, my duty to that imaginary entity
> the working class seemed the most doubtful of abstrac-
> tions. I began to notice what neglected, neurotic waifs the
> children of so many Communists were, and to question the
> genuineness of a love of mankind that didn't begin at
> home.[62]

Joy noted that one Soviet novel that she reviewed for *New Masses* "had a heroine who let a Nazi commander shoot her newborn baby rather than betray her comrades." Joy examed her own feelings in the face of such a dilemma: "I knew I would do otherwise, and let the comrades take care of themselves. Perhaps it was reality coming in to displace imagined reality."[63]

However one analyzes it, Joy's commitment to family surpassed loyalty to Party and revolution. By November 1943 Joy reviewed few films at all; that task went to her successor, Joseph

Foster. Her contributions after that were occasional book reviews and poems. Her final book review appeared on July 10, 1945, and her last poem was printed in the magazine three weeks later. After April 1946, her name, which had appeared in one way or another since the advent of World War II, was dropped from the list of contributing editors.

By the time Joy's association with *New Masses* ended, she was, for all intents and purposes, no longer a member of the Communist Party. Never again did she go to Party meetings, and she stopped writing for the revolution. For her, as for many idealistic and angry younger Americans, the Communist Party had changed. "During the Depression, an honest anger at injustice and misery had brought many able and generous" people into the Party. But she admitted that after 1945 "a renewed faith in America, and dismay at the antics of the Soviet Union, took them out again." Disillusioned now, she still had no ideological alternatives to the Party.

> By 1946 I had two babies; I had no time for Party activity,
> and was glad of it; I hardly mentioned the Party except
> with impatience. And yet, out of habit, I went on believing
> that Marxism was true. Habit, and something more. For I
> had no knowledge of divine help, and all the world had lost
> faith in gradual progress; if now, in the day of the atomic
> bomb, I were to lose my trust in violent means of creating
> heaven on earth, what earthly hope was there?[64]

Nearing the end of World War II Thomas Yoseloff edited a slender volume of antifascist, antiwar poetry. Joy Davidman contributed seven pieces. Only one of these was at all lively, and it had been published years earlier in *Letter to a Comrade*. The title of Yoseloff's book was *Seven Poets in Search of an Answer*.[65] Joy was indeed wandering, searching for an answer. Teaching, Hollywood, four summers at the MacDowell Colony, numerous friends in the world of writers, the Communist Party—not one of these experiences gave her life lasting satisfaction or meaning. In desperation, she sought ever more fulfillment in her marriage. In fact, both she and William Lindsay Gresham were venturing upon self-renewal projects. Joy was, after all, twenty-seven years old when they married in August 1942. It was time that she grew up, left the protective cover of home, and ventured out on her own. She knew that, and her parents did, too, but Joy wasn't certain how to begin. The opportunity to marry Bill Gresham seemed like the perfect solution. She could leave home without being completely alone, and transfer her attention and energy from the Communist Party to husband and family. Here was a way to ease gracefully out of the Party and find something meaningful to fill the void.

However, if Joy had searched systematically for the wrong mate, she could not have improved on William Lindsay Gresham. That was not apparent in the beginning; everyone who knew Bill Gresham said he was a charmer. He enjoyed being around people and was a witty storyteller. He possessed a deep, lusty, baritone voice, conveying, along with his dark eyes and body language, a sensuality that appealed to Joy's sense of eroticism. The lean six-footer was seductive, and Joy reveled in that, craving a permanent, meaningful relationship with a man who had a healthy sexuality. Bill was also very bright, a free-lance writer, a Communist, and a Spanish Civil War veteran. He was an outspoken nonconformist, and perhaps most important of all, he was a lost soul—an almost defeated seeker who needed someone or something to cling to.[66]

Six years older than Joy, Bill was born in Baltimore, Maryland, on August 20, 1909. His parents, who were lower-middle-class Southerners from eastern Maryland and Virginia, moved to New

York in 1917. Nine years later he graduated from high school in Brooklyn. A curious blend of Southerner and New Yorker, Bill could turn a Southern accent on and off at will. He enjoyed imitating backwoods evangelical preachers and did it so well that some people assumed he had been one.[67] Although he loved the cosmopolitan character of New York, especially Manhattan's East Side, he clung to certain Southern ways. His individualistic approach to life was manifested in his singing folk music in Greenwich Village night spots. And while Bill had a good voice and people enjoyed hearing his songs, the appeal of folk music did not reach the great metropolis until World War II, making this avocation rather singular. It was part of an image that he cultivated with diligence.

After high school Gresham supported himself by singing in Village clubs at night; he took a few college courses during the day. Then in 1933, with money tight and even part-time jobs difficult to find, he joined the newly created Civilian Conservation Corps. About two years later, Bill married a New York woman wealthy in her own right, and he set out to become a writer. The *New York Evening Post* finally took him on as a book reviewer and movie critic, but only after an apprenticeship as an office boy. Because he never really overcame that stigma, he left the *Evening Post* after only a few months, going to work for a fledgling Manhattan advertising agency. By late 1936, he had abandoned that position too, determined to go it on his own as a free-lance writer.

Precisely how his first wife reacted to this drifting is uncertain, but Bill found an excuse to get away from her and his still-unsuccessful writing career by joining the Abraham Lincoln Brigade and heading off to Spain as a freedom fighter during the civil war. Bill volunteered to take the place of a close friend killed in the battle of Brunete as a supporter of the Spanish Republic.

When Bill returned to New York two years later, the freedom
fighters had been defeated and he himself was a broken man. Bill
was suffering from alcoholism; his marriage—although not for-
mally dissolved until early 1942—was ruined; and he had a mild
case of tuberculosis. To make matters far worse, he was on the
verge of a nervous breakdown. Recalling the years between 1939
and 1942, when he married Joy Davidman, he wrote,

> I met a social worker who knew what a neurosis was, and
> through her I got to an expert psychoanalyst after two years
> of disintegration and despair. I snatched at love; when my
> health improved, I snatched at writing; I did a little work for
> left-wing writers' organizations. And I tried to control my
> own mind by will power; diamond cut diamond. Finally,
> since my mind was only "a function of matter in motion"
> and since it was filled with nightmares, I decided that this
> painful motion had gone on long enough. I hanged myself
> with a leather belt, to a hook in a closet.
>
> Whether it was an accident or the intervention of a
> Power greater than myself, I shall never know in this life. At
> any rate, I came to myself on the floor—the hook had
> pulled out of the wall.[68]

Apparently unable even to kill himself, Bill allowed a friend in
the Communist Party to introduce him to a psychiatrist. The ana-
lyst was a Freudian, and he promptly enrolled the shattered man
in lengthy analysis that eventually spanned several years. Through
analysis Bill came to believe that he had been severely scarred by
his parents' divorce. When he was sixteen, his mother and father
had separated. "My father got a small apartment less than a mile
from where we lived in Brooklyn and for seven years I never saw
him; he was too proud to ask me to come to see him and I was too

shy to ask if I might!"[69] Bill was also plagued with a horrible case
of acne, and this left him with more scars than those on his face.
He came to believe people shunned him because of his scars, and
consequently he spent hours in front of a mirror looking at himself, talking, and practicing being charming.[70]

It was with this disturbed but enthralling man that Joy Davidman fell in love in spring 1942. In August the pair went to Joy's
favorite retreat in New Hampshire to be married. It was a beautiful summer Sunday afternoon, August 2, when Joy and Bill called
on a justice of the peace in Peterborough. They were married by
him and then they went over to the MacDowell Colony, where
Marian MacDowell helped to supervise an outdoor reception. The
gala was attended by a group of politically radical and literary
friends of the newlyweds and by the bride's brother and parents.
Howard was in medical school in New York by this time, so he was
able to attend the big event, and Jen and Joe, despite their dismay
over Joy's rather hasty marriage to a virtually unemployed writer
who was also a gentile and a Southerner, came and put on their
best faces. Actually, it was not terribly difficult for them to do so,
because Bill was warm and engaging; and at least he was not a
practicing Christian.[71]

The honeymoon ended soon after it started. The impoverished couple moved to a tiny flat on East 22nd Street, and Joy continued to work at *New Masses*. Her twenty-five dollars-a-week
salary was not much, but it was more than Bill was earning as a
free-lance writer. To be sure, he was writing, but he had sold nothing longer than short stories; and those were few and far between.
His drinking was a major obstacle to sustained literary effort, but
he saw a deeper neurosis as the problem.

Despite Joy's hostility to psychoanalysis, Bill was sold on the
benefits of therapy and proceeded to go back into analysis. This
strained the marriage for more than one reason: Joy viewed analy-

sis with a jaundiced eye, and the increased strain on the budget made the subject still more controversial.

To get Bill away from the company of old friends who enticed him into the drinking establishment at the Dixie Hotel, which was at that time a hangout for carnival people, the couple moved to a three-room apartment in Sunnyside, Queens. In less-than-spacious quarters, and with anywhere from two to six cats, they began to raise a family in a neighborhood that Bill called a "human filing cabinet."[72] Joy gave up her associate-editor position, and on March 27, 1944, the first child, David, was born. Seventeen months later, November 10, 1945, Douglas entered the Gresham family. By now, even if they had gotten rid of the cats—and Joy always loved to keep cats—the Sunnyside flat was too small. With their few pieces of furniture and a library of some two thousand books, they moved again.

Joy had reasons for moving other than the cramped quarters in Queens. She felt a need to be closer to the wilds of nature. The outdoors had nurtured her as a youngster in Maine, and the trees and mountains of New Hampshire had revived her spirits during recent summers. And there was yet another impetus behind the move: Bill was having an extramarital affair, and Joy wanted to get him as far away from that particular temptation as possible.

She coped with his infidelity by pouring out her emotions in verse. Indeed, the last poem she had published in *New Masses* reflected her sorrow and hurt as much as her political leanings:

> Houses are quiet at evening. The sad colors
> are sliding down the cypresses. Quiet, quiet.
> Eyes look out of the sky, and the roof hides you
> But the house is quiet. . . .
>
> (but you meant no harm did you and there was nothing
> else you could do was there and they promised order

a new order and you thought they would win
and there was a standard of living to maintain and a
    blonde
and you were afraid. . . .)[73]

For a variety of reasons, then, Joy severed her last ties with *New Masses* and the Greshams moved to Ossining, a town situated on the Hudson over twenty miles north of the city. This Westchester County community was a fair distance from the crowd and noise of New York City, and it had become a fashionable address for a group of young literati and professional people. One woman who lived there in 1946, and who knew Joy and Bill, put it this way: "Many had moved up from N.Y.C. and were liberal, leftist, radical—choose one—and interested in causes." With the hindsight of more than thirty-five years, and amusement at their youthful idealism, Helen Walker Puner wrote, "I don't really remember what the hell it was we thought we were promoting—possibly some sort of cultural exchange with Russia? In any event, we held monthly meetings in a large, drafty old Victorian house on Ossining's Main Street. The light inside was crepuscular; the heat in winter, non-existent. Joy and her husband would show up," Puner continued. "They were *very nervous* people. Very high-strung. I used to think that if I talked to her, she would run away in fright. They didn't literally shake but they seemed to be shaking anyway. (Perhaps Gresham was a drinker?) She was fragile, unbelievably intense. It must have cost her a great effort to come to meetings—she was very far away from being a public person. I guess the reason I hesitated to talk to her personally was that I felt I might be invading her privacy."[74]

There were tangible causes of this dangerous change in Joy's personality. Not only did Joy have the strain of two babies, Bill's drinking and unfaithfulness, and constant worry about money, to cope with—but also the fact that Bill was rapidly approaching a mental collapse. Joy saw this coming but was helpless to do anything about it. His breakdown came just a few months after they settled into Ossining. Joy wrote, "One day he telephoned me from his New York office—I was at home in Westchester with the children—to tell me that he was having a nervous breakdown. He felt his mind going; he couldn't stay where he was and he couldn't bring himself to come home. . . . Then he rang off." Joy spent the rest of the day frantically making phone calls and trying to locate Bill through his friends and acquaintances. "By nightfall there was nothing left to do but wait and see if he turned up, alive or dead. I put the babies to sleep and waited. For the first time in my life I felt helpless."[75]

Chapter 3

THE CRISIS, THE SEARCH, THE ANSWER (1946–1953)

"All My Defenses . . . Went . . . and God Came In"

By 1946, there was a large crack in Joy Davidman's protective armor. Brighter and better educated than most people, more widely read than the majority of college-educated adults, and certainly an accomplished writer for a person thirty-one years of age, Joy had never entertained weakness or failure. She even rationalized the Hollywood fiasco in a way that allowed her to perceive herself as unbowed. But Joy's arrogance, acerbic wit, and frequent abrasiveness could not cover her fear of loneliness and failure. Acquaintances at Ossining had observed a strikingly more quiet and contemplative person than the Joy who criticized books, poetry, and movies for *New Masses*: the incredibly high level of self-esteem ingrained in her by her father was rapidly fading.

Bill's unfaithfulness had been devastating enough to Joy's gigantic ego; his breakdown was shattering. The prospect of supporting herself and her children on her meager royalty checks was almost more than she could bear at the moment, and the thought of crawling back to her parents in an admission of defeat was humiliating, especially since they had counseled against her marriage.

C. S. Lewis once remarked that "every story of conversion is a story of blessed defeat," and if anyone was defeated it was Joy Davidman Gresham after receiving Bill's desperate call. By night-fall the babies were quiet and in bed. No one else was in the apartment. There was no one left to call. Joy was alone with herself, her fears, and the quiet. She confessed that "for the first time my pride was forced to admit that I was not, after all, 'the master of my fate' and 'the captain of my soul.' All my defenses—the walls of arrogance and cocksureness and self-love behind which I had hid from God—went down momentarily—and God came in."[1]

Joy described her perception of God in this way:

> It is infinite, unique; there are no words, there are no comparisons. Can one scoop up the sea in a teacup? Those who have known God will understand me; the others, I find, can neither listen nor understand. There was a Person with me in that room, directly present to my consciousness—a Person so real that all my precious life was by comparison a mere shadow play. And I myself was more alive than I had ever been; it was like waking from sleep. So intense a life cannot be endured long by flesh and blood; we must ordinarily take our life watered down, diluted as it were, by time and space and matter. My perception of God lasted perhaps half a minute.[2]

During this intensely spiritual episode Joy was stunned to find herself on her knees, praying: "I must say I was the world's most surprised atheist."[3] To her astonishment, the formerly ardent materialist not only knew that God was there, but that He "had always been there" and that He loved her.

Such was Joy's conversion experience. She said she repented, "God came in," and "I changed. I have been turning into a different person since that half minute."[4]

Anticipating the criticisms of materialists such as her father, Joy emphatically argued that her encounter with the living God "was no comforting illusion conjured up to reassure me about my husband's safety." Although "my surprise was so great that for a moment it distracted me from my fear; only for a moment, however." Soon "I was just as worried . . . as before. No; it was terror and ecstasy, repentance and rebirth."[5] As she expected, "People have since argued that it was natural for me to invent a comforter at such a time, that it proved nothing. The flaw in that argument," she continued, "is that I got no comfort. I was just as worried about Bill afterward as before."[6]

That night in early spring 1946 changed her life. She was never the same again. The Damascus Road-like experience made her "aware simultaneously of the blinding presence of God and my own personality, black and smudgy, as I had never seen it before. I admitted my own arrogance, my intolerance, my prejudices, my vindictiveness. All in half a minute—it would have taken years of psychoanalysis."[7] Gradually, confidence returned; she stopped shaking and exuding fear. Her new confidence was built upon a loving God rather than on her own or her father's concept of iron will and self-reliance.

Bill came home several days later to find his wife a changed woman. While she was deeply concerned about him and thankful that he was safe, she emanated a striking serenity that he had never seen in her before. Joy promptly told Bill about the presence of Another in their room. "He accepted my experience without question; he was himself on the way to something of the kind." Bill's life, after all, was a disaster. He was out of control. Since Joy had obviously found something that might benefit him, he was open to the search. "Together," Joy wrote, "in spite of illness and anxiety, we set about remaking our minds. For obviously they needed it. If my knowledge of God was true, the thinking of my whole life had been false."[8]

Joy began living out the parable of the pearl of great price. She surrendered all to acquire the precious gem. Her quest for a clearer focus on the God she met became an increasingly consuming goal, almost an obsession. "I could not doubt the truth of my experience," she conceded. "It was so much the *realest* thing that had ever happened to me! And, in a gentler, less overwhelming form, it went right on happening. So my previous reasoning was at fault, and I must somehow find the error."[9]

Joy acknowledged that she "was by no means a Christian at first; all my atheist life I had regarded the 'apostate' with traditional Jewish horror." To clarify her vision she consciously tried to revive her commitment to Marxism—at least to Marxian economics. She thought this would help others. In her quest she read Marxist theory, in depth, for the first time. "It was a difficult and painful study. Inch by inch I retreated from my revolutionary position; fallacy after fallacy, contradiction upon contradiction, absurdity upon absurdity turned up in Lenin's *Materialism and Empirio-Criticism*," and in other works that were the guidebooks for radicals.[10] Why she had not read Lenin and the other radicals in greater depth before, she never said.

If Marxism was a blind alley for the Jewish woman who found apostasy abhorrent, the logical next step was Judaism. She decided "to become a good Jew, of the comfortable 'Reformed' persuasion." But Judaism proved a dead end for her as well. Although in Judaism she felt closer to belonging, the Person she met, the One who continued to nudge her, was still absent from this tradition. Ultimately, she failed to find in Judaism any recognition of what she now believed she had received; in her words, "the conviction of sin followed by the assistance of God's grace."[11]

In the midst of their search for a new life the Greshams enjoyed a brief respite from their perennial problem of poverty. In 1946 Bill's first novel, *Nightmare Alley*, was published and dedicated to Joy. The book is a gruesome tale, interwoven with tarot cards and murder, about an alcoholic who becomes a carnival geek (a person who supports his drinking habit by biting heads off live chickens to entertain sideshow clientele).[12] The advance and royalties on *Nightmare Alley* were used to take care of day-to-day expenses and to pay some creditors, but the real excitement came when Bill's agent (Bill was represented by Brandt & Brandt now, too) negotiated a motion picture contract for it. Overnight, the Greshams had more money than they had seen between them in years.

They agreed that the $60,000 stipend from Hollywood should be used to buy a house and land in the country. Joy wanted the money to be invested in a roof over their four heads, in a woodsy setting, before Bill had a serious drinking relapse and did something foolish with the cash. Bill had always dreamed of owning a farm with a big house, so Joy had no argument from him on this score. To him the country place would be a mark of success, proof that he had finally arrived. His grandmother, a woman to whom he had been closer than his own "rootless and distraught" mother, had taught him that her "ideal of a perfect man" was General Robert E. Lee. Bill recalled that from her he gained a desire to "try to be exactly like him."[13] A spacious house in a rural community, especially one with white columns, green shutters, and a veranda overlooking the grounds, would definitely suit the needs of this dreamy descendant of former slaveowners. And this is precisely what the newly rich couple found, fifty miles north of Ossining. At

Pleasant Plains near Staatsburg, the Greshams located an old white-columned mansion with fourteen rooms, green shutters, and a second story front veranda. Situated on twenty-two acres of timbered land were also several outbuildings, some cultivated garden land, and plenty of woods for strolling and gathering firewood.[14]

Joy delighted in her new surroundings. Picking wild strawberries and mushrooms, and digging up edible roots soothed her, as did gathering fruit from their trees and planting and harvesting vegetables. Each year at the farm she canned enough fruit and vegetables to supply the four Greshams for the winter with enough left over to give parents and friends.[15]

While almost Thoreauvian in veneration of nature, Joy loathed housework. The grounds and garden gave her immense pleasure, but housekeeping in such a large abode was not to her liking. "The real trouble," she argued, "is that housework is too easy, too boring. There is no sense of achievement from wiping floors and washing dishes."[16] No one ever accused her of hypocrisy on this matter. Cousin Renée was appalled by the poorly kept house, and one visitor from the area was struck by the lack of care given to the mansion's interior. Although there was the grand piano, which Joy had owned since the early 1930s, and hundreds of books adorning the built-in shelves, "the house Joy and her husband lived in was a grim place. The living room was sparsely— almost Spartanly—furnished. . . ."[17]

Neither was the attractiveness of the Gresham domain enhanced by the great number of family pets. Always the cat lover, Joy kept as many as fourteen felines on the premises at one time. During inclement weather they were housed in the storm cellar, and if unsuspecting guests witnessed the opening of that portal, they were frequently overcome by the sight of more than a dozen cats of all colors and sizes emerging from the darkness, clamoring for food. The pungent odor that such an army of cats created was always enhanced by those of one or two dogs. Topsy, a brown canine of unidentifiable breed, had been found injured on the road and nursed back to health by the family. Topsy not only survived the roadside ordeal, but gave birth to a litter of puppies; one of the brood was kept for a pet. Dubbed Brownie by the boys, the pup was eventually upstaged by another, found and christened Blackie.[18]

As Joy cooked and sewed for her family and oversaw their large menagerie, she diligently sought to know the God she had met at Ossining, devouring books in search of clarity and insight. A long poem by English poet Francis Thompson, entitled "The Hound of Heaven," had a large impact on the seeker. Earlier Joy had ridiculed it "as a piece of phony rhetoric—but, understanding it suddenly, burst into tears." Not only was her understanding of "The Hound of Heaven" new, the crying was new, too. "I had seldom previously cried except with rage."[19] It is little wonder Thompson's poetry touched Joy, since much of her life's journey was captured in the writer's verse:

> I fled Him, down the nights and down the days;
> I fled Him, down the arches of the years;
> I fled Him, down the labyrinthine ways
> Of my own mind; and in the mist of tears
> I hid from Him, and under running laughter.
> Up vistaed hopes, I sped;
> And shot, precipitated,
> Adown Titanic glooms of chasmed fears,
> From those strong Feet that followed, followed after.
> But with unhurrying chase,
> And unperturbèd pace,

Deliberate speed, majestic instancy,
They beat—and a Voice beat
More instant than the Feet—
"All things betray thee, who betrayest Me."[20]

The works of C. S. Lewis had an even greater impact on Joy than Thompson's. Before she met Lewis, she wrote: "I snatched at books I had despised before. . . . I went back to C. S. Lewis and learned from him, slowly, how I had gone wrong. Without his works, I wonder if I and many others might not still be infants 'crying in the night'" [21] Joy was particularly influenced by Lewis's *The Great Divorce, Miracles: A Preliminary Study,* and *The Screwtape Letters.*

As important as Thompson and Lewis were in Joy's quest to know her God better, neither had the authority and power she found in the Bible. After reading all sorts of things, and then sifting, sorting, searching, and doing it again, she knew: "And the Redeemer who had made Himself known, whose personality I would have recognized among ten thousand—well, when I read the New Testament, I recognized him. He was Jesus."[22]

Once Joy took the leap of faith and became that apostate she had always dreaded, she discovered that "the rest was fairly simple. I could not doubt the divinity of Jesus, and, step by step, orthodox Christian theology followed logically from it."[23]

This was 1948, and Joy, Bill, and the boys (David was three and Douglas one and a half) began attending church. Their choice at that time was not based upon denominational preference or doctrinal position; instead they sought the closest Christian church to their home. In those days, Joy maintained "that one should worship along with one's neighbors, not go far afield in search of 'kindred spirits.' The church nearest my . . . home in Dutchess County, New York, happened to be Presbyterian; I visited it and found its theology suited me well." Bill agreed, and Joy and the boys were baptized that year in the Pleasant Plains Presbyterian Church. Bill joined the church with them on confession of faith. He liked what he was seeing in Joy, and he wanted to change.[24]

In 1946, Joy abandoned atheism for faith; in 1948, she moved from faith to commitment. A key person in Joy's transformation from believer to committed disciple was C. S. Lewis. However, she probably would never have met the Oxford don had it not been for Dr. Chad Walsh. Joy first learned of Chad Walsh's interest in C. S. Lewis in 1948. Walsh, a professor at Wisconsin's Beloit College and an ordained priest of the Episcopal Church, was a young man who was already established as a poet and critic. The summer Joy and the boys were baptized, Dr. Walsh published an article in *The New York Times Book Review* entitled "A Variety of Writers—and How They Rediscovered God."[25] This piece shed some light on Lewis, as had Walsh's earlier essay in *The Atlantic Monthly*, "C. S. Lewis, Apostle to the Skeptics."[26]

Prior to Walsh's interest in Lewis, no one had taken an intelligent, in-depth look at the life and writings of the British Christian apologist. Eva Walsh, Chad's wife, urged him to expand his *Atlantic* article into a book-length study. With her encouragement, he began the research and writing, and then filled in some gaps through a series of interviews with Lewis during the summer of 1948. The Beloit professor acknowledged that "via transatlantic airmail [Lewis] had urged me to desist and devote my time to better subjects (such as some safely dead writer), but once he became convinced that I considered the study worth doing he wholeheartedly cooperated with me."[27] Macmillan brought out Chad Walsh's splendid book, *C. S. Lewis: Apostle to the Skeptics*, in 1949. This volume, plus the earlier essays, firmly established Chad Walsh as the foremost American authority on the Oxford scholar—a fact not lost on Joy Davidman.

By this time, Joy had passed the frightened, tremulous period. Her relationship with Christ had restored her confidence and vigor. During the months of her depression and near-collapse, she had been able to do little more than care for the two boys and read detective stories.[28] By the time of her baptism, however, she was reading voraciously (C. S. Lewis and Charles Williams in particular) and was at work on a novel in which she could put art to work again—but now for the cause of Jesus Christ rather than Karl Marx and world revolution. Revitalized and bursting with enthusiasm for her new way of life, Joy began reaching out to find people with whom she could discuss theology and her new interests. During this period of growth Joy discovered that doctrinally she was an Episcopalian rather than a Calvinist, and she changed churches. Bill and the boys followed suit.

The most significant and lasting friendship that Joy made at the time was with Chad Walsh. Their correspondence began in June 1949, and a camaraderie started that was to last until Joy's death eleven years later. Joy wrote and expressed interest in Lewis, explaining how much his writing had affected her conversion and was influencing her forthcoming novel, entitled *Weeping Bay*. Joy suggested that the Walshes and Greshams get together that summer, and she invited Chad and Eva to come and stay with them at Staatsburg. The Walshes had no car, but they were taking the train to Vermont, where they were vacationing for two months. At Chad's invitation, Joy and Bill went north and spent a week with the Walshes, inaugurating a summer tradition that continued until Joy moved to England in 1953.

Eva Walsh found Joy to be "very bright. When you first met Joy she was plain looking, but after you knew her she was attractive." To Chad, "there was nothing feminine about her," nor did he find her particularly attractive. Yet, "Joy was one of the most intelligent people I ever met. She had a finely honed mind—almost frighteningly intelligent," and this seemed to overshadow any other early impressions.[29]

Jacqueline Jackson, well known today as a writer of children's fiction, met Joy at Lake Iroquois in Vermont, in summer 1950 or 1951. Jackson was an impressionable young college student at the time, and she was captivated by Joy's energy and enthusiasm. An aspiring writer herself, Jackie Jackson talked to Joy at length and went on strolls with her around the lake and through the woods. The compelling strength of Joy's personality is still remembered by Jackson. Joy had become an authority on mushrooms, and while hiking she would swoop down on an umbrella-shaped fungus, examine it quickly, and pronounce its Latin name. Then she would describe to Jacqueline the subtle flavor peculiar to the variety, and thrust it to her face with a command to eat it. Cognizant of the dangers of eating poisonous toadstools, Jackie would view the fleshy morsel with apprehension. But Joy's personality was so magnetic that Jackie would devour the mushroom because it seemed far better to risk death than to offend her brilliant mentor.[30]

If Joy was glowing, Bill, too, had changed for the better. By summer 1949 his second novel, *Limbo Tower*, was out. A story based on the time he spent in a tuberculosis sanitorium after the Spanish Civil War, this book was more optimistic in tone than *Nightmare Alley*; the new tone generally reflected his improved mental health during this early period of spiritual development.[31]

Despite his somewhat disheveled appearance and the slight stoop to his six-foot frame, he enthralled people with his wit, charm, and storytelling. Bill had traveled all over America, and he had seen much of Europe. He had a stream of anecdotes about the people he had encountered along his various journeys.[32] Chad Walsh remembered Bill as "delightful to be around; a wonderful raconteur." Nevertheless, he seemed immature beside Joy; he demonstrated less depth of character and knowledge.

Joy "was sure of what she believed, and she loved to take people on in debates. She was argumentative, and she spoke with contempt for those she felt were superficial thinkers." She "disliked modern poetry—especially the trend toward irony." And after reading one of Chad's books of poetry she chided him for employing irony, and urged him instead to "tell it straight." Joy delighted in talk of literary criticism, and she spent hours discussing theology and general Christianity. She regaled Chad with accounts of her conversion and mystical experiences, although he was reticent to probe the latter subject because of its intensely personal nature.[33]

During that first summer's meeting, one of the central topics of conversation was, of course, C. S. Lewis. Inasmuch as Chad Walsh had interviewed Lewis twelve months earlier, he was able to assure Joy that the don was most approachable, a gentleman who would readily respond to a letter from Joy, who was a serious student raising penetrating questions.

Joy wanted very much to write to Lewis, but for some reason— perhaps fear of being presumptuous—she did not post a letter to him until the following January. Indeed, Lewis's brother, Major Warren Hamilton Lewis, noted the date of the letter in his diary. Major Lewis observed that "until 10th January 1950 neither of us had ever heard of her; then she appeared in the mail as just another American fan, Mrs. W. L. Gresham from the neighborhood of New York. With however," the Major noted, "the difference that she stood out from the ruck by her amusing and well-written letters, and soon J[ack] and she had become 'pen-friends.' "[34]

As soon as Joy received her first reply from C. S. Lewis, she dashed off a letter to Chad with the good news:

> Just got a letter from Lewis in the mail. I think I told you I'd
> raised an argument or two on some points? Lord, he
> knocked my props out from under me unerringly; one shot

to a pigeon. I haven't a scrap of my case left. And, what's more, I've seldom enjoyed anything more. Being disposed of so neatly by a master of debate, all fair and square—it seems to be one of the great pleasures of life, though I'd never have suspected it in my arrogant youth. I suppose it's *unfair* tricks of arguments that leave wounds. But after the sort of thing that Lewis does, what I feel is a craftsman's joy at the sight of a superior performance.[35]

The correspondence Joy initiated and continued with Lewis was now a high point in her life. Except for Stephen Vincent Benét in the past, and Chad Walsh more recently, Joy quite honestly had not found intellectual equals with similar interests. While Bill most certainly had a first-rate mind, he did not quite measure up to Joy's level of genius—few people did. This had never really hindered meaningful communication between them. However, by 1950 their relationship was once again ailing, and Joy thirsted for challenging intellectual stimulation.

The ever-widening gulf between Joy and Bill was caused by many factors. First of all, Joy dived more and more deeply into her commitment to Christianity, while Bill's devotion to the cause of Christ grew ever more shallow. His public announcement of conversion, which was published in *These Found the Way* in 1951, was written in late 1949; it was two years old when it came off the press. An analysis of his experience, when compared with Joy's testimony in the same book, shows his to be so close to hers that it must be labeled derivative.[36] Perhaps it would be unfair to say that Bill borrowed his account from Joy; Bill was, after all, a talented writer who had original ideas, and he wrote every bit as gracefully as his wife. However, Joy remained a Christian throughout her life, whereas Bill wrote to his son, David, a few years later: "I am not a Christian and will probably never be one since I cannot understand the basic doctrines nor accept them."[37] This was a curious thing for a man who had embraced the beliefs expressed in the 1951 publication to write. In any case, time proved Joy's testimony to be real and lasting; Bill's was only temporary.

Bill Gresham's growing away from Christianity is a real-life example of Christ's parable of the seed falling on rocky soil. His faith had sprung up quickly in the shallow soil, but it died early because there was no root. Bill's belief was superseded early by other religions and cults. Chad Walsh described Bill as a maverick, or a drifter, a man who couldn't seem to stay with any one thing for an extended time. This had been demonstrated in 1949 when Joy and Bill first met the Walshes in Vermont. Bill, although newly converted to Christianity, was ecstatic about Ron Hubbard and his philosophy of Dianetics [Scientology]. Bill tried to pull Joy along these lines, too, but after a brief flirtation she rejected the pseudo-science as harmful to her Christian discipleship.

Bill continued to dabble in Dianetics long after Joy abandoned it; he also plunged into Zen with a ferocity that knew few bounds. His discovery of this Buddhist sect pulled him still farther from Christianity. In January 1950, Joy wrote a four-page, single-spaced letter to Chad Walsh, a letter brimming with excitement over new Christian insights she was gaining; Bill scrawled the following note on the end of the epistle:

Hey Chad—

Do you know anything about a weird and wonderful worldview called "Zen"? Started in China (called *Ch'an*), from Buddhism, developed in Japan. Fascinating stuff. Will tell more later if you are interested. And I want to write to Lewis about it. It may have something we can use.

Bill[38]

Tarot cards and yoga also occupied Bill's time, as did a new interest in the I Ching. These "spiritual quests," as he labeled them, coupled with his interest in Zen and Dianetics, left him no room for Christian growth at a period when Joy was spending an increasing amount of time and energy reading scripture and books on Christian doctrine, and generally trying to become a devoted disciple of Jesus Christ.

The wedge separating the couple was driven still deeper by other factors. Joy had earned two college degrees; Bill had never finished college. This was always a point of friction in their relationship. Likewise there was competition between them as writers. But these problems were not major, and under normal circumstances, could have been solved. When added to other woes, however, they assumed gigantic proportions. Perhaps because Bill came out of a family where antebellum planter traditions were venerated, he had a nineteenth-century view of a woman's role in marriage. Bill wanted to treat a woman as an object to be loved, petted, and, of course, dominated. An insight into his attitude toward women may be found in a letter to a creative-writing teacher who had asked him about one of his novels:

> Perhaps you would be interested in some "husband lore" which I have picked up during the years: If you take a wife out somewhere and she suddenly turns cross (without you having flirted with some other gal), either she has started to have her period unexpectedly or her shoes hurt. Most women appreciate coffee in bed of a morning more than a mink stole. When men are tired they grow silent. When women are tired they tend to chatter. A good husband must know when to be his wife's father as well as when to be her son.

. . . By keeping track of his wife's menstrual cycle he
can tell when to suggest TV dinners instead of an elaborate
meal. A menstruating woman cannot time a cheese soufflé,
or let an impatient word roll off harmlessly. No woman can
find a spare handkerchief in a sad movie—husband should
always carry a spare. And an experienced husband always
carries aspirin for headaches and band-aids [sic] for shoes
that pinch or cut.[39]

Bill went on to point out that he wrote this to the teacher not to
impress her with "how smart I am, but because I thought maybe
your students might be interested in how a fiction writer observes
his fellow men—and women."

What the teacher and students saw in the letter is not as important as imagining how well Joy Davidman lived under this yoke.
Even assuming that this gulf of misunderstanding could have been
bridged, there were many more blows to stagger their relationship.
Bill was an alcoholic, and he could not stop drinking. Despite
repeated attempts to give up liquor, as well as half-hearted ventures
into Alcoholics Anonymous, he seldom stayed sober for more than
a few days at a time. Sometimes his drunkenness was manifested in
violence: one night he shot a hole in the ceiling to display his anger,
and on another occasion he hit one of the boys in the head with a
bottle. He threw a pie at the ceiling one evening, and once, while
strumming his guitar on the porch and growing impatient when
his alcohol-numbed fingers couldn't pick out the correct chords, he
twirled around in a fit of rage and smashed his instrument to pieces
on one of the front porch columns. Howard Davidman was confident Bill never intended to harm anyone during these outbursts,
but, rather, enjoyed being theatrical to attract attention.[40]

Whatever the motive, the most devastating blow to the marriage
came with Bill Gresham's continuing infidelity. Soon after his self-

styled conversion to Christianity, the hard-drinking novelist, trying to fill the empty space inside himself with liquor, also sought satisfaction in a string of extramarital liaisons—short-lived affairs and one-night stands. Bill never tried to hide these indiscretions, and he could not understand why Joy was so hurt by them. On the contrary, he took a macho pride in these encounters. Without shame or remorse, he told Chad Walsh one summer in Vermont that "a guy has to recharge his battery every so often."[41]

Joy could cope with the multitude of differences between them, but the unfaithfulness was more than she could handle, especially when, in February 1951, Bill turned to another woman while Joy was sick and unable to be physically intimate. This so devastated Joy that she moved into her own bedroom at the opposite end of the house. From that time on, as far as she was concerned, one dimension of their partnership was over.[42]

A turning point in Joy and Bill's life came early in 1952. Joy's first cousin Renée came with her two children to stay at Staatsburg. Renée, five years younger than Joy, had known her cousin since childhood; her mother, Rose, was Joseph Davidman's sister. Like Joseph, Rose was born in Europe and emigrated to America as a child. Rose grew up in New York City, and there she married a Cuban Roman Catholic; eventually the couple went to Cuba to live, and Renée spent her early years on the island. Her parents divorced when she was an adolescent, and Renée was taken back to New York City to live with her mother and the Davidman family.[43]

During World War II, Renée married Claude Pierce and moved to Alabama. Pierce, like Bill Gresham, was a drinking man. Unlike Bill, though, Pierce was almost always violent when he was drunk; his outbursts were routine rather than remarkable. By early 1952, Renée had reached the end of the line with Claude, but she knew he would never let her leave or give her access to enough money so that she could run away while he was at work. One day she concocted a liberation scheme. Assuming that Claude would allow her to go to her mother if the woman were ill, she wrote Rose in New York, begging her to send a telegram, saying that she had suffered a heart attack and needed Renée at her bedside.

Rose cooperated, and the telegram came. Renée got Claude's blessing for the trip and said she would take the two children (Bob, aged five, and Rose Mary, aged three) because he could not care for them and work, too.

Renée arrived in New York City knowing that Claude would come after her once the ploy was revealed. She had to go into hiding. Her husband knew nothing of Joy and Bill, since he had never even met them, so Rose called Joy and asked if she would put up her cousin and children until a permanent solution could be found. Joy was most agreeable. The next day Bill picked up Renée, Bob, and Rose Mary, and escorted them on the train from Manhattan to Dutchess County.

When the destitute and bedraggled trio arrived, Joy met them with hot food and drinks and opened her home to them. Renée said Joy's generosity was touching, but not out of character. Only recently the Christian convert had taken in two children of a couple suffering from alcoholism. Joy and Bill were always ready to help unfortunates, even when finances were tight.

Joy and Renée got on well together, although they saw the world from markedly different angles of vision. Renée, who had attended Hunter College but never graduated, had a first-rate mind, but she was no intellectual and did not aspire to be one. Renée preferred being a full-time mother and wife (if possible), and she placed a high priority on keeping a clean, orderly house.

No one suggested that Joy did not love her two boys, or that she was not a good mother.[44] Nevertheless, Joy valued writing and gardening, and she let things inside the house slip. When Joy decided to cook, she could compete with the best of chefs. Much of the time, however, she was content with simple fare; she slept in occasionally and encouraged the boys to make their own breakfasts, usually cold cereal.

When Renée arrived, she found that the Greshams employed a woman three days a week to clean the house and do laundry and ironing. She soon took over much of the cooking. This was a way that she could help recompense her benefactors; it was something she enjoyed doing when Joy was in a writing mood. Renée came to assume an increasing share of the washing, ironing, and cleaning, especially when money became short several months later.

Renée and Joy had different views about clothing, too. Renée was always carefully and stylishly dressed; her children wore color coordinated clothes, and their shoes were never without polish. Douglas and David were frequently less than impeccable in their dress, and Joy enjoyed going about Staatsburg, Rhinebeck, or Poughkeepsie with black Mary Jane shoes, white socks down at the heels, wrapped in an old coat that was fastened with safety pins where the buttons had fallen off. Being with Joy on such occasions embarrassed Renée, but Joy seemed to enjoy her image as the local eccentric writer.

The cousins had differences other than housekeeping and dress code; their views of religion were equally divergent. While Joy was becoming steeped in her Christian spirituality and trying to tell her houseguest about her mystical experience and newfound faith, Renée, who had been raised a Roman Catholic, made it clear that she no longer had use for religion of any kind.

Despite the differences, however, the two cousins got on quite well. Renée shared one of the twin beds in Joy's bedroom, and they spent hours late at night talking. For several months they talked incessantly, and no doubt both benefited from this impromptu therapy. Joy was able to open up to Renée, describing how Jen had always praised Renée as the model youngster, properly dressed, graceful, with invariably perfect manners. Joy was able to overcome her resentment of Renée, admitting that the situation was not her cousin's fault. Indeed, Joy could even see that much of her own Bohemian dress and behavior over the years had been a way to rebel against her mother by being as different from Renée as possible.

Admitting her anger was spiritually and psychologically beneficial to Joy. In fact, she not only felt better emotionally, but began to change her personal appearance. No longer finding it necessary to resent Renée, Joy was free to imitate the qualities she liked in her cousin. Renée was immaculately clean and stylishly dressed, her hair beautifully groomed and her figure striking. Joy, who had allowed herself to grow dumpy after two pregnancies, and was hardly a model's delight in personal appearance, began to lose weight, regain her youthful shape, and improve her choice of clothing. By summer 1952 Joy had totally discarded her Greenwich Village radical image. In its place emerged an attractive woman of thirty-seven, with a handsome figure.

Renée, too, derived good from this time with Joy. She had found a refuge for herself and the children, and personal support during the painful crisis in her marriage. Furthermore, Renée began to learn something about alcoholism. Bill was on the wagon again, and to support his effort Joy went with him to at least one meeting of Alcoholics Anonymous a week. Frequently, they took Renée with them to AA, and she began to understand what was plaguing Claude and how it was affecting her and the children.

Sadly, there was explosive tension between Bill and Joy even though he was no longer drinking. His writing was not going well. Joy felt he was not writing enough, and their money was dwindling fast. There remained, also, the problem of Bill's continuing infidelity. He still could not understand why Joy should take it so personally, and he found her shutting him out of her bedroom unforgivable.

Joy was in an intolerable position by summer 1952, or so, at least, it seemed to her. A sober Bill was easier to live with than a drinking Bill, and as Renée phrased it, "Joy knew that a sober Bill earned more money." While these motives were undoubtedly there, loftier ones were present, too. Now that Joy was a Christian—and one most certainly influenced by C. S. Lewis's view of divorce and marriage—she no longer believed in divorce, and she felt compelled to do everything possible to salvage her marriage. Furthermore, she did love Bill, who was still as shattered inside as when they first met. His psychological distress—he always said he suffered from neuroses—brought psychosomatic disorders, among them severe, chronic cases of eczema and asthma.

Bill was an insecure man in need of constant reinforcement and praise. While she did love him, Joy also feared and loathed him, and therefore she found it impossible to give him the vast amount of support he needed. Joy wrestled with her choices. Should she stay with Bill? This was apparently her Christian duty. On the other hand, scripture permitted her to abandon the marriage because of Bill's adultery. And what about the boys? Was it wrong to take them from their father, or was it worse to have them live with him when on more than one occasion, he had been violent and hurt them? In 1953 Joy recalled that by summer 1952, "I was so much under Bill's influence that I had to run away from him physically and consult one of the clearest thinkers of our time for help."[45]

That thinker was C. S. Lewis. Although Lewis was the breadth of the Atlantic Ocean away and money was scarce, Joy was determined to go see him, and she knew Renée could help. Now that the cousins were on good terms and genuinely trying to assist one another, Joy asked Renée to care for Bill, the boys, and the house while she made the pilgrimage to England.

Renée agreed. After all, she, Bob, and Rose Mary were still living with the Greshams, and the three of them had no place to go without being discovered by Claude. Besides, Renée still wanted time to decide what to do about herself and her marriage. Staying on, as the housekeeper and mother, so to speak, gave Renée an opportunity to remain for a while without in the slightest being a burden.

Joy could list several reasons for the trip without airing the Greshams' marital problems in public. First of all, she had always loved English history and literature; a trip to Great Britain had been a lifelong dream. With Renée's generous assistance, such a trip was now possible without disrupting the boys' schooling. Secondly, because of a recent and serious bout with jaundice, Joy's physician had urged her to get away from everyone for a time and rest. If these reasons weren't adequate, Joy had another rationalization; she had a manuscript to prepare for the publisher, and she needed time alone to complete the task.[46]

Joy sailed for Liverpool from New York in August 1952. With a partially completed manuscript in hand, she immediately set to work to finish *Smoke on the Mountain: An Interpretation of the Ten Commandments*, a nonfiction book with a decidedly Christian message.

Smoke on the Mountain was not Joy's first venture into witnessing to her Christian faith. Ever since she had acknowledged the divinity of Jesus, sought forgiveness for her sins through His atoning death, and then set out in faith to become a committed disciple, she had felt a need to tell others about God's love as it had been revealed to her. Joy experienced a great healing through Jesus

Christ—healing from fear, bitterness, and despair. Her life had meaning and direction for the first time, and she wanted to share her discovery with others.

Her first attempt to speak of her faith publicly came in 1949, when she was approached by Oliver Pilat of the *New York Post*. Pilat wanted to do a multipart feature on Joy, tracing her journey from Communism to Christianity. She finally agreed to help the reporter with the article, which appeared between October 31 and November 13, 1949, but only after prolonged agony and prayer. Certainly Joy had always been a public person; in one way, telling her story was an opportunity to make her mark with a new identity. However, this was not the primary impetus. The truth is that she almost refused Pilat because she knew that her testimony would anger some people, and certainly embarrass many friends and relatives. Incurring the wrath of a few people did not bother Joy, but she did not relish hurting her loved ones.

Joy suffered immensely because of her brother's reaction to the *Post* story. When Howard learned about the proposed series, he implored Joy not to do it. He used every means of rational persuasion at his disposal. Finally, he beseeched her as her brother—out of loyalty to him personally—not to publish this confession. Ultimately Joy decided to proceed with "Girl Communist," but in deference to Howard the lengthy autobiography did not even mention him. This, Joy hoped, would protect him from any fallout that might harm his private practice in psychiatry.[47]

Joy explained her major reasons for going on with publication in the conclusion of the series. She maintained that inasmuch as she had made a "mistake in public," she should "admit it in public." Furthermore, "I must have had some [effect] on some people," therefore, "if describing my own history of error could do anybody any good, I decided that's what I ought to do." Finally, and primarily, she wanted to bear witness to the power of the living God. "In short," she concluded, "I was willing to look like a fool for the greater glory of God!"[48]

Joy certainly paid dearly for her stand. What she saw as being "willing to look like a fool" for Christ's glory was viewed by many others as playing the buffoon. Her former colleagues at New Masses viewed the revelation with jaundiced eyes, and one close friend lamented that "the lengths she went to in her public recantation . . . were a sad spectacle."[49] Most devastating to Joy, though, was her brother's reaction. Howard refused to see her. Although he did— finally—correspond with her once he learned she was terminally ill, they never looked upon one another again, or talked about those years when they were so close and compatible and stood side by side against their father and the world.

Joy stood without Howard to face her father and mother after this article was published. But Joe and Jen were not angry, and that was probably the most difficult thing for Joy to bear. This time they did not see Joy's behavior as youthful rebellion like joining the Communist Party. Instead, they now saw her as mentally disturbed; and they were deeply saddened that she was choosing, in their eyes, such an inferior solution to her problems.[50]

Despite the pain Joy suffered from her confession and the Post series—and she was no masochist—she continued to tell her story to anyone who would listen. When David Wesley Soper decided to edit a volume entitled These Found the Way, a collection of spiritual autobiographies written by midlife converts, Joy agreeably submitted an article on her journey from materialism to Christianity, and she concluded her account by announcing that she wanted "to serve God in books and letters as best I can."[51]

To this end, Joy wrote a novel that she hoped would inspire others to turn from whatever shackled them to the freedom of life in Jesus Christ. Entitled Weeping Bay, the 257-page book was placed with Macmillan by Joy's agent. Set in Quebec's Gaspé Peninsula, the book tells about life in a fishing village that has a small factory where stoves, plows, and barrows are manufactured. M. Evangeliste Boisvert, the condescending and greedy factory owner, exploits his workers but pretends to be a good Catholic. The village priest is controlled by the manufacturer, because he has the money to support the priest, church, and rectory in unobtrusive luxury. When an idealistic young priest, the Abbé Desrosiers, comes to Weeping Bay with lofty plans for improving the plight of the workers through unionization, the inevitable conflict develops between capital and labor, between the parish priest and the young radical.

Weeping Bay is an ambitious novel with several important themes, and Joy also used it as a pulpit to preach several sermons of her own. She criticized the conservative wing of the Roman Catholic Church severely for what she believed to be antiquated and myopic views on birth control, marital sex for pleasure, and penance. She excoriates the corrupt parishioners who think they can buy forgiveness while practicing sin and the priest, who lives in comfort at the expense of his parishioners. The meaning of the twenty-first chapter of the Gospel according to Saint John, where Christ says, "Simon . . . lovest thou me? . . . Feed my sheep," is a recurring theme throughout the novel, as is the end of innocence. Finally, not only the corruption of the parish priest and the businessman have been exposed; the young cleric is revealed to be more concerned about building a union than in truly "feeding the sheep." False gods of all kinds are unveiled in *Weeping Bay*, and finally the recognition occurs as Desrosiers is praying on his knees before a stone statue of the Virgin Mary. Broken spiritually because his union has been crushed, the abbé begins to recite "Hail Mary, full of grace, the Lord is with thee. Blessed . . ." Just then a vision of Jesus appears to the heartsick priest:

"Child," said the Carpenter, "why not pray to Me?"

Desrosiers bent his head silently. "I am afraid of you, Lord," he answered in the terrible honesty of the innermost mind. "Your mother only comforts and forgives; it is easy to pray to her. But you have said what you would have us do. I cannot do it. I am afraid." . . .

"No man can serve two masters [Jesus said], for either he will hate the one, and love the other; or else he will hold to the one, and despise the other. Choose therefore."

"Have I not chosen?" Desrosiers' thoughts said desperately. "Once for all, and long ago?"

"No. Choose now."

[But] Desrosiers denied his vision. . . . He said aloud, clearly, "These experiences, as the Church tells us, are often sent to us as temptations of the Devil."[52]

To no one's surprise, few reviewers were neutral about *Weeping Bay*. Critics either spoke highly of the novel, or they condemned it out of hand. Granville Hicks in *The New York Times* wrote "I have no idea what the sources of Miss Davidman's knowledge are, but she convinces me that here is part of the reality behind the much-admired picturesqueness of the Gaspé. It is a dark picture that she has drawn—and one that bears the marks of authenticity." In the *New York Herald Tribune*, James Hilton wrote that "Miss Joy Davidman shows how much can be done by care, competence, a point of view and an unusual geographic background. [She] has told her story straightforward and with a sharp eye for detail." Despite her "severely critical attitude toward the Catholic Church," he continued, she is "not blankly or blindly hostile; and her portrayal of the degree of difference possible inside of the field of clerical opinion is revealing enough to be plausible."

Some critics did not share Hilton's opinions. Mary Sandrock for the *Catholic World* dismissed it as a story "told with a large case of made-to-order characters in quick, spasmodic incidents. Unfortunately, however, it takes more than pamphleteering and sight-seeing to make a novel." Even harsher was R. P. Breaden in *Library Journal*, who attacked the book as "marred by obscenities and bursts of blasphemy . . . in spite of the excellent descriptive passages."[53]

Weeping Bay did not sell well, but its plight is evidently less the result of poor reader acclaim than internal politics at the publishing company. A year after the book was published Joy wrote to Kenneth Porter:

> I hope you like *Weeping Bay*—if you can find a copy. The book was quietly suppressed at Macmillan's home office by an ardently Catholic sales manager, for reasons you'll understand when you read it. They've since fired the guy and sent me an implied apology, but too late to do me any good. Oh, well, here's a chance for me to practice Christian forgiveness, if I can stop gnashing my teeth long enough. . . . [54]

Such opposition by no means forced the strong-willed Joy Davidman to retreat from the battle. On the contrary, it made her resolve to launch a counteroffensive with new tactics. Rather than make her appeals to spiritual seekers through the novel, she determined to write nonfiction for Christian publishing houses, thereby avoiding the problems encountered with *Weeping Bay*. The plan came to fruition in *Smoke on the Mountain*, the manuscript she finished on the long-yearned-for trip to England.[55]

While Joy did achieve her writing goals in England, of much more importance to her was meeting the man she had come to consider her mentor: C. S. Lewis. Their initial introduction had taken place through the mail, but the first face-to-face meeting came in the dining room of the Eastgate Hotel, across from Magdalen College, Oxford. It seems that Joy had a "pen friend" in London before she had ever corresponded with Lewis; the friend's name was Phyllis Williams. When Joy decided to make the trip, she arranged to stay with this woman. In early September Joy and her companion invited Lewis to the Eastgate for luncheon, and he accepted.

Returning the favor, Jack, as his friends called him, invited Joy and Phyllis to have lunch with him and his brother, Major Warren ("Warnie," to those close to him) Lewis, at Jack's rooms at Magdalen College, where Jack taught. At the last minute, Warnie backed out of the luncheon, so Jack, who was very shy around women, contacted his good friend and former student, Professor George Sayer of Malvern College, and asked him to take Warnie's place.

George accepted the invitation and had a delightful afternoon. He remembered that they dined on salmon mousse for the main course, and that Joy kept the conversation flowing any time there was a lull. Sayer recalled that Joy was slim and well dressed; her clothes were quiet and tasteful, and her makeup was discreet. Most impressive was her brilliant wit. When Sayer inquired her impressions of England, her responses were artfully expressed and extremely funny, and "Jack laughed uproariously."

After lunch, Lewis took everyone on a tour of the college. Walking most of the time in pairs (Jack and Joy were together), chatting about England, the United States, and English literature, the foursome had a pleasant afternoon replete with good food, stimulating conversation, and laughter.[56]

Apparently, Joy Davidman made a favorable impression on the Oxford don; soon he invited her back to Magdalen College for lunch. This time he arranged for her to meet Warnie and two or

three colleagues. Warnie noted the occasion in his diary, acknowl-
edging that he "was some little time in making up my mind about
her; she proved to be a Jewess, or rather a Christian convert of
Jewish race," and he found her rather attractive, of "medium
height, good figure, horn-rimmed specs, quite extraordinarily
uninhibited." During this luncheon, the Major recalled that Joy—
he referred to her as Mrs. W. L. Gresham—"turned to me in the
presence of three or four men, and asked in the most natural tone
in the world, 'Is there anywhere in this monastic establishment
where a lady can relieve herself?'" This behavior was bold at best,
and crude at worst; but there was enough pungent humor in it
that Warnie could conclude, "Her first visit was a great success,
and a rapid friendship developed."[57]

It is likely that Joy was already falling in love with C. S. Lewis.
Renée believed that her cousin had fallen in love with Lewis's
mind during their extended period of correspondence, and since
Joy's marriage was a shambles, it does not require an overly active
imagination to believe this. Lewis perhaps was growing infatuated
with Joy; at least he delighted in her company, or he never would
have continued the round of luncheons. But Joy was a married
woman, and neither she nor Lewis could do more than fantasize
about what the future might hold for them.

Warnie, too, found Joy enthralling. This is evident by his diary
entries and by the invitation he and Jack both offered to her to
come and spend a fortnight at the Kilns—their home—just before
she returned to the United States.

The two weeks Joy spent at the Kilns was a heady time for all
three of them, despite Jack's worry about how to entertain their
American guest. Bathroom facilities in particular concerned the
bashful bachelor. He discussed her impending visit with a married
man, his friend George Sayer, and inquired precisely how they

should arrange things for her comfort and entertainment. It was Sayer's counsel that they behave as usual, continuing their routine of reading, writing, walking, and pub calling.[58]

Having a woman houseguest was a singular event for these two unmarried writers, and that they did it at all underscores their desire to have the pleasure of Joy's company. In any case, the visit went off without a snag, and Warnie observed that Joy "liked walking, and she liked beer, and we had many merry days together."[59]

Joy informed Chad Walsh about the holiday with Warnie and Jack in fascinating detail:

> First chance I've had to write to you—so much has been
> happening. I stayed with Jack and Warnie over a fortnight
> just before I sailed for home, and had a marvelous time; by
> the way, they both send their love. Quite an experience it
> was, Christmas with the Lewises! (An enormous turkey, and
> burgundy from the Magdalen cellars to go with it; I stole a
> wineglassful to put in the gravy, and they thought it was
> practically lese majeste—till they tasted the gravy.) Being
> on vacation, Jack was taking life easy—he was merely writ-
> ing his book on prayer (it's going to be a wonder, I've read
> part of it), correcting OHEL [Oxford History of English
> Literature] proofs, setting scholarship and fellowship exam
> papers, doing a college edition of Spenser for an American
> publisher, and finishing the *seventh* Narnia book . . . also, of
> course, answering the endless letters. This left him time to
> go over my own Decalogue [*Smoke on the Mountain*] book
> with me (about 50,000 words of it) and tell me how to fix
> it; he liked it quite well, thank Heaven. Also there was a lot
> of walking and talking. One day the three of us went over
> Shotover to Horspath and then to Garsington, coming back
> by way of Wheatley (do you remember all those places?)

and getting caught in a savage rain—I blistered my feet,
and Jack and Warnie practically had to pull me up over
Shotover on the last stretch. But it was great fun.

I even got taken to a Christmas pantomime, where we
all roared enthusiastically at the oldest jokes and joined in
the choruses of the songs. I'll never forget Jack coming in
loudly on something that went like this:

> Am I going to be a bad boy? No, no, no!
> Am I going to be awful? No, no, no!
> I promise not to put some crumbs in Aunt Fanny's bed,
> I promise not to pour the gravy over Baby's head. . . .
>   etc.

I wish the critic on Presbyterian Life who objected to my
quoting of Yeats' The Fiddler of Dooney ("The good are
always merry") could have heard that!

And, of course, the pubs—Eastgate and Bird and Baby
and the Ampleforth (up in Headington) and lots of others.
Some day I'm going to open a pub in Oxford. I've become a
complete Anglomaniac anyhow, can't wait to transplant;
I've never felt at home anywhere as I do in London or
Oxford. And after the magical gold light of the English
landscape, ours looks strangely flat and dull to me.

—The OHEL volume is going to make people sizzle,
it's full of controversial stuff and reversals of conventional
judgments. I am the *first* person to see those galleys, and I
feel very honored. By the way, I also read a lot of Jack's
poetry and I think you're wrong about it. It's quite new and
strange and unfashionable, a complete break with the modern conventions of intellectual and bloodless verse, and for
that reason rather difficult to appraise it; but I thought a lot

of it was damn good. Technically it's amazing. He's used
very old forms and given them an entirely new twist. (He
liked *my* poetry too—so there!) But you and I will never
see eye to eye on verse.

I'm in fine shape now and all set to do lots of writing.[60]

It had been a marvelous respite, with Joy dedicating *Smoke on
the Mountain* "To C. S. Lewis" for a Christmas present, and Lewis
presenting her with a copy of George MacDonald's *Diary of an Old
Soul* dated and inscribed by MacDonald on April 27, 1885, and
with Lewis's inscription to Joy which read: "Later: from C. S.
Lewis to Joy Davidman, Christmas, 1952."[61]

Joy's saying that she "can't wait to transplant" to Chad Walsh
and Jack's inscription to "Joy Davidman" rather than "Joy Gresham" might be lost on people who did not know what had tran-
spired at the Kilns a few days before Joy left for home in early
January 1953. Bill Gresham had written a four-page, single-spaced
letter to his wife just before she sailed for the States:

> You have written several times that you can't understand
> the cool tone of my letters and have wondered what
> makes. I didn't think the letters were cool but if I under-
> stand you right, you have wanted me to say definitely what
> was going to happen when you came home. I wanted to
> get things clear in my own mind and I also felt letters can
> do just so much as they are no substitute for personal dis-
> cussion. Also I didn't want to cloud your holiday with
> things that would upset you.
>
> Renée and I are in love and have been since about the
> middle of August. [Joy sailed in early August.] If it had not
> been for our love I could not have come through this sum-
> mer with as little anguish as I have for things have been
> rough financially.

Bill went on to say that there were many unpaid bills, including some related to Joy's trip to England, and this burden had added to his problems. He assured Joy that the children were doing well, but they were "missing you more than they usually admit." Regarding their marriage, Bill acknowledged

> I understand, I believe, what resolutions you have made
> about coming home and trying to make a go of our mar-
> riage. But I feel that all such decisions are sacrifices of
> human life on the altar of Will Power, with the women's
> magazine hacks serving as high priests. I have never yet
> know[n] will power and determination to "make a go of
> marriage," to take the place of life in its complete sense. I
> have tremendous affection for you and have certainly
> missed you, although I was glad that you were having fun
> and adventures and seeing all the things you wanted to see.
> But affection and intellectual comraderie [sic] are not mar-
> riage. People who are fond of each other and respect each
> other and set out to "make a go of the marriage" for the
> sake of the children are setting up a situation of constant
> affinity enforcers and reality deniers.

Bill reminded Joy that she could never be anything but a writer, whereas "Renée has a different orientation; her only interest is in taking care of her husband and children and making a home for them." Because Bill assumed he could never earn enough "to hire a staff of servants to handle the cooking, the cleaning, and the child care so that you and I can both have careers as writers," he envisioned no future for the continuation of their marriage. The "optimum solution," in his eyes, "would be for you [Joy] to be married to some really swell guy, Renée and I to be married, both families to live in easy calling distance so that the Gresham kids could have Mommy and Daddy on hand." Bill did admit that "obviously there is the question of your cooperation in this ideal solution."

Because Bill knew of Joy's opposition to divorce on Christian grounds, he strongly argued that *he* saw nothing "sinful" in his proposal. And in any case, "when physical attraction is gone from a relationship between a man and a woman, all the comradeship in the world will not bring it back, and between you and me it is gone and has been gone for years." Concluding the unpleasant subject he wrote: "I am more than willing to take full responsibility for this if it is a question of responsibility. But people cannot fall in love by will power and they certainly cannot fall back in love by it."

Bill ended the letter on a philosophical note, urging Joy, "If you feel lost, forsaken and unloved, Poogle," to "just try to remember that there are a vast horde of lock chains that remain to be scanned off your case. . . ." The reference was to a Dianetics process. Finally, he wrote somewhat coldly, "I don't think it will be practical to take the boys down to meet the boat."[62]

Joy showed this letter to Lewis soon after it arrived, and the two of them discussed her predicament. "I asked Lewis for advice," she told Chad Walsh, and he "strongly advised me to divorce Bill."[63] On this note Joy left England, no doubt indicating to Jack that if the marriage in fact was dead, she might return to Britain with the boys and start a new life.

"I can't let her go back to that awful place," Lewis informed George Sayer. He was referring to the United States; Joy had spoken derisively of her country's rampant materialism and foreign and domestic polity. Certainly Jack had Bill Gresham and the house in Staatsburg in mind, too, but he was too much of a gentleman to discuss Joy's personal life without her permission. At first Jack did not even tell Warnie of Joy's crisis; and when she departed, the Major noted only that "when she left for home . . . it was with common regrets, and a sincere hope that we would meet again."[64]

When Joy arrived back in Staatsburg, she found the New York weather bitterly cold—and that Bill was drinking again. As soon as Joy had left for Great Britain, Bill announced to Renée that he was "cured" of his alcoholism, and that he could begin social drinking once more. Because Bill's alcoholism was not manifested in a constant stream of vileness and violence, like Claude Pierce's, Renée persuaded herself that Bill's drinking was under control; if he overindulged once in a while, it was only because he was nervous about ending his marriage to Joy.[65]

For a time Joy kept her marital burdens largely to herself; only Lewis knew the extent of the problem. Even Joy's first letter to Chad Walsh after England contained no mention of the domestic trauma she, Bill, and Renée were enduring at the upstate farm. But, by late February Joy could no longer hide her agony. She wrote a long letter to the Walshes and poured out her heart. Without venom she announced that "Bill and I are on the point of divorce, more or less by mutual agreement. I can't pretend I'm sorry." She confessed that things had been miserable between them for years "and my conscience wouldn't let me quit." Upon learning about Bill and Renée, Joy admitted to being "rather shattered at first, but [I] have now decided it will be a blessed release."

Joy summarized her view of the problem, and prefaced it with a request for counsel on the problem of divorce:

> I don't know how you feel about divorce. I always took it
> that divorce was only the last possible resort, and felt I
> ought to put up with anything I could bear for the chil-
> dren's sake. And I hoped that Bill's adulteries, irresponsibili-
> ties, etc., would end if he ever recovered from his various
> neuroses; also that his becoming a Christian would make a
> difference. Unfortunately I've been disappointed on both
> counts. Bill gave up being a Christian as soon as he found

out it meant living by a moral code and admitting and
repenting one's sins. And now that he is reasonably stable,
cheerful, and energetic as a result of Dianetics, he feels
ready to go out and paint the town red. In a way I can see
how he feels—for so long he was unable to enjoy life at all,
and what with anxiety and psychosomatic ailments, that
now he's like a man just out of prison and off on a bender.

Joy placed no blame on Renée for the collapse of the marriage,
but conceded that she should have known Bill would make
advances toward Renée. In any case, the relationship was devastated before Renée arrived.[66]

Renée stayed on with the Greshams until she could get
enough money together to go to Florida and file for divorce. "We
parted very good friends," Joy wrote and "I *did* tell her" to stop
feeling guilty because "I felt it would be a blessing for me in the
end. . . ."

Joy confided in the Walshes about the reception she received
in New York: "Bill greeted me by knocking me about a bit. . . .
Two days after he'd half choked me, he asked in all seriousness,
'Have you ever known me to do a brutal or unkind thing?'" She
mentioned to Chad and Eva that since she had come home, Lewis
had urged her more strongly to leave Bill; and because of her mentor's prodding and Bill's strong-arm tactics, "now I'm rid of the
feeling that it's my duty to go on!"[67]

Although Joy acceded to Bill's wishes for a divorce, the divorce
could not take place soon because they were too broke to hire a
lawyer. Back taxes were due on the house and income tax was due
to Uncle Sam; royalty checks were too small to cover expenses.
"Things are improving," she reported to the Walshes, "and I hope
to get away within a year at the most."

Divulging that England was her destination, Joy wrote, "I hope to take the children . . . and bring them up there—not so much because I'm completely in love with England, though that's part of it, as because living is so much cheaper there and I'll be able to live decently on what Bill can pay. Knowing him," she mused, "I'm very doubtful whether he will pay for long; but perhaps I can sell enough stuff myself, through my American agent, to keep going no matter what."[68]

Joy neglected to mention to Eva and Chad Walsh that C. S. Lewis was the most powerful attraction for returning to Britain, but perhaps she didn't have to spell out what was already obvious to everyone who knew her well.[69]

Joy Davidman, December 1915.

Joy and Howard Davidman, early 1920s.

Joy Davidman, winter 1921.

Joy and Howard Davidman, August 1931.

Joy Davidman, 1933.

Bill Gresham, 1941.

The Greshams, about 1950. Left to right: Joy, David, Bill, Douglas.

The Greshams' farmhouse at Staatsburg, 1949.

Bill and Renee Gresham with Rose Mary and Bob, late 1950s.

Joy Davidman, 1951.

At right, Old High Street, Headington, Oxford.

C. S. Lewis with David (*left*) and Douglas Gresham at the Kilns, 1957.

Joy at the Kilns, about 1957.

Joy Davidman Lewis, 1960.

C. S. Lewis in his study at the Kilns, August 1960.

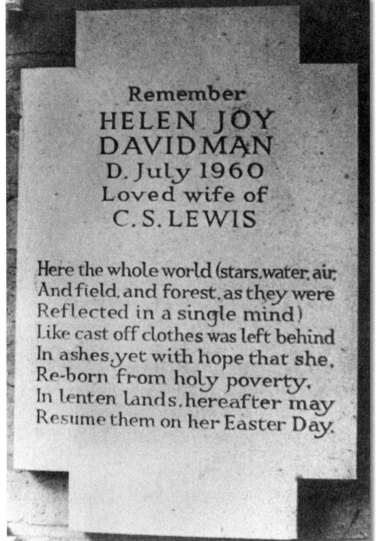

Remember
HELEN JOY
DAVIDMAN
D. July 1960
Loved wife of
C. S. LEWIS

Here the whole world (stars, water, air,
And field, and forest, as they were
Reflected in a single mind)
Like cast off clothes was left behind
In ashes, yet with hope that she,
Re-born from holy poverty,
In lenten lands, hereafter may
Resume them on her Easter Day.

Joy Davidman's memorial, with inscription by C. S. Lewis,
Headington Crematorium.

Chapter 4

MIRACLES, PAIN, PEACE (1953–1960)

"I Think I'm Going Somewhere by God's Grace, According to Plan"

I don't like England, Mommy." These were the first words nine-and-a-half-year-old David Gresham spoke when the Cunard Line's M.V. *Britannia* docked at Liverpool.[1] David's mood was colored by rain and the gray sky that November day in 1953, and he was also hurt by his family's breakup and the sad farewell to his father in New York. David never changed his mind about England; nearly three decades later he wrote from his home in Switzerland, "I suffered a lot from my parents' divorce and my subsequent exile in England."[2]

Douglas, who had celebrated his eighth birthday aboard ship, was not certain how he felt about England. He, too, missed his father, and he had grown rather fond of Renée and her children. But Britain was an adventure, and eventually he viewed Oxford as the only real home he had until he married and relocated in Tasmania, Australia.[3]

Joy felt a touch of sadness, too. She wrote to Bill a couple of days after their arrival that "when we left you were so sweet that I found myself beginning to trust you again."[4] Those parting feelings changed nothing, though, because Renée finally got Claude to accept the fact that she was not coming back. By autumn 1953 Renée's divorce was final. The following August 5 Joy and Bill's divorce, which Bill had filed for in Miami on the grounds of desertion and incompatibility, was legal, and Bill married Renée that same day.

Joy felt twinges of ambivalence about leaving New York because of the boys and Bill, and she also knew she would miss her parents. Despite the pain that was inextricably bound up in her relationship to them, she did love her parents. Besides, the boys had served as buffers between parents and grandparents. The periodic family visits in New York were not exactly delightful for Joy, but she and her parents got on much better now than ever before. Things had long been improving between them because, as she told Chad Walsh, "since my first discovery of (or by) God," her parents "had lost their old power to hurt me." Certainly they could still "rattle me a bit," but after a 1950 visit Joe and Jen made to the farm Joy said, "for the first time I was able to laugh wholeheartedly and feel wholehearted pity. . . . Keep up the prayer, please, please!"[5] Finally for Joy, there was hurt over leaving America without seeing Howard. On cold, drizzly, and dark days, such as the one on which they touched shore, Joy must have asked herself if she had made the correct choice in leaving family, friends, and homeland behind.

Over two years earlier Joy had made a decision to turn her will and life over to the care of God. She still made mistakes and fell out of God's will from time to time, but she did not deliberately practice sin. Her hair-trigger temper still exploded periodically; in fact, repenting and seeking God's help to keep anger under control was one of Joy's greatest struggles. The hot temper was a demon with which she contended for years on a daily basis.[6] But all imperfections aside, Joy had the inner peace of knowing, as she phrased it, that she was "going somewhere, by God's grace, according to plan."[7]

Joy was being led by the Spirit, and that reality was manifested in her ability to cope with her parents' peculiarities and with Bill's desire to make his future with Renée. Her spiritual growth was also evident in her clear understanding of scripture in a classical Christian sense and in the rapidity with which she acquired a mature systematic theology. Joy's concept of original sin and personal accountability was set forth a few months before she sailed for England:

> . . . I am coming to think that the easy diagnosis of "neurosis," whenever anybody behaves badly or irrationally, is an outgrowth of humanist and Utopian thinking about the nature of man. That is, most moderns feel that man is naturally good; therefore a "healthy" man, by their definition, is a perfectly good one, and all sins are illness which can be cured! Also they don't allow for individual differences at all; the word "normal" has been perverted into a synonym for "healthy." We who know there's such a thing as original sin must find it tragicomic to see so many people paying thousands of dollars to self-appointed experts of the mind, in order to be "cured" of being human. . . . [8]

The divinity of Jesus Christ was at the center of any theology worth labeling "Christian," she proclaimed to fellow poet Kenneth Porter. The "$64 question," to Joy's mind, centered on Jesus. "Was he God or wasn't he?" She elaborated on the centrality of this question by emphasizing that "No amount of talk about Jesus' saintly ideas will help if we don't think he's God; for if he was just another human, then he could be mistaken like the rest of us, and his ideas are just his private whims, as ours are." She went on to point out that we all have to decide on what authority "we call his ideas saintly." If it is by God's authority, "How do we know what God thinks (except through what Jesus told us, and unless Jesus was God he was just guessing)." Disputing those who label Jesus "a good man," she argued that such a position "really means only that we like him because he agrees with *us*—and the minute he doesn't agree with us we will toss him overboard. . . ."[9]

Eternal life as humankind's hope was laid out by Joy in Pauline terms: "And one's whole approach to life, one's whole philosophy, turns on this point." If there is no other life than this one, our goal should be to enjoy it as much as possible, ignoring any pretext of duty. "But if there's something yet in store, then our goal" is to make ourselves living sacrifices to Christ for His kingdom. "Not, God help us, because we *like* suffering, or because it's a good thing in itself! Of course it isn't; whereas pleasure *is*. But because we must become beings of perfect love and selflessness; because the walls of the self are walls shutting out God." Joy went on to agree with Saint Paul that if we are wrong about heaven, "'Then we Christians are of all men the most miserable.' Because then, you see, the only real good would be the good things of this world— which Christians must often give up."[10]

Combining her views on original sin, perfectability, and eternal life, Joy logically concluded that, "As a Communist I used to be optimistic about the species and pessimistic about individuals." Now, as a Christian, "that is reversed. I'm pessimistic about the species, but optimistic about individuals."[11]

Joy's reasons for assuming the veracity of the Gospel accounts of Jesus' life are so intricate and typical of the way her mind worked that they must be quoted at length:

Reporters and cops develop a sixth sense for recognizing a liar in the flesh; professional writers can sometimes tell one

in print. It's partly one's knowledge of psychology—for
instance, if the Apostles had been romancing they would
never have told so many stories which made them look silly.
Nor would their immediate followers. They would have
said, "We knew Him when, we were the extra-special faithful ones who understood Him perfectly, we were the ones
appointed to govern the rest of you!" If they had lied, they
would have been lying for their own advantage, surely?
Instead of which—continual rebukes, and "He that would
be first among you [sic] let him be last!"

And similarly—and in addition to Lewis's reasoning on
this point—anyone who thinks Jesus could have been a
paranoid with delusions of grandeur has only to read up on
real paranoids, in the asylum and out, and see what they
sound like. History is full of self-appointed Messiahs, and
they all sound the same, mad with pride. The humor and
common sense of Jesus never came from a disturbed mind.

But mostly, I think, what convinced us was our sense of
the difference between fiction and life. Fiction is always
congruous, life usually incongruous. In fiction there is a
unity of effect, of style; the people all say exactly what they
should say to be in character and in the mood. And all the
effects are heightened, arranged. If there is an incongruous
reaction, that too is obviously arranged—either for humor
or for some plot reason; and it looks as blatant as a movie
double take.

Lies, being planned, have that same congruousness and
extra effectiveness—they're all of a piece. But in real life
one has no time to plan, one merely reacts; and the reaction
is likely to be ever so slightly off key, inapposite. Like Lady
Macbeth when they tell her Duncan's been murdered:
"What, in our house?"

Hardly anyone but Shakespeare could have brought that off; and, even so, perhaps he was using something he'd heard. For the remark is that of an innocent woman. A guilty one, with time for preparation, would have launched into three yards of high-grade fustian.

Well, the Gospels are full of these little incongruities— like the cut-off ear of the high priest's servant. That's a thing that happened, no one could have invented it. The account of the Virgin Birth, not being eyewitness, seems on the other hand an invented and composed story, without a single false note. Everyone strikes exactly the right attitude, from Mary's first words to the Angel on through that beautifully composed artistic climax. How artistically the contrast between the Prince of Peace and the Manger is worked out!

Whatever actually happened (and, frankly, I consider the Virgin Birth not unbelievable but merely irrelevant) the story as we have it is a work of art. But the eyewitness accounts are quite otherwise. Details an inventor would fill are lacking; details a faker would suppress are there. That touch about all the scraps picked up after the loaves and fishes miracle! A faker in the grand manner would have loftily ignored the scraps as undignified; couldn't the miracle worker always make more? It's just the sort of illogical thing that *really* happens. You can see them saying, "We musta dreamed it. But, golly, looka all them scraps!" A writer clever enough to understand the force of such a corroborative detail, I think, would have written the rest of the story with more drama.

And the little dead girl who's resurrected: a faker would have had Jesus tell her to pray, and, like as not, the story would have been rounded off with a touching household thanksgiving service. But Jesus simply tells the family to

give her something to eat. That *Happened*. The man who
could have invented it would have been greater than Shakespeare. And the blind man who sees people, after the miracle like trees walking.

And, most of all, the Resurrection. The women who
mistake Jesus for the gardener! The general slowness to rec-
ognize him, and Thomas's insistence on a material demon-
stration . . . in fact, the Apostles are always remarkably
materialist. People talk as if they were creduluous men in a
primitive and credulous age. But the age was anything but
primitive—decadent rather, wasn't it, and very like ours? Its
excrescent cults of phallic worship and divination and
astrology were exactly what we've got today, and, as today,
the great majority of people were hard-headed materialists;
if they listened to fortune-telling, it was not for the wonder's sake but in hope of getting a business advantage. And
the Apostles always seem to come from Missouri.

I could mention other things—for instance, there's just
the *right* amount of discrepancy in the eyewitness stories.
And there's the intangible of style; the personality of Jesus
is luminous in everything he says. I've met oafs who con-
tend that Jesus escaped somehow from the cross, retired to
Patmos, and grew up to be St. John! I find it incredible that
anyone should be so unaware that the style's the man. To
mistake the bitter, humorless, florid, and fanciful poet of
Revelations [sic] for Jesus . . . but then, there are serious
scholars who work hard at proving that Bacon wasn't
Shakespeare, without ever noticing that one conclusive fact
that, simply by the kind of man that comes through
Bacon's writing, he couldn't have been Shakespeare.

But mostly it's just that I know the sort of thing that
people make up, and this ain't it. I suppose that's what

Lewis feels too, when he says we couldn't have invented it, and also what Tertullian meant when he said Credo quia impossible. [Joy probably meant *Certum est, quia impossibile est*.][12]

Joy also concluded that once she realized her relationship to her great God, she was able to care less what other people thought of her actions. If she believed she must behave in a certain way to please her Lord, then so be it, regardless of how foolish it might appear to earthlings. Being a fool for God was not merely all right, but liberating. She wrote that she "found that out when . . . looking back at the arrogant, brash kid I used to be, and writhing with regret over the impression I must have made on people—when suddenly I asked: Who am I, that I shouldn't look like a fool?" Then she added that she "Felt much better at once!"[13]

"In His will is our peace," Joy liked to quote,[14] and she made a herculean effort to live by that credo. Going to England looked so foolish to family and many friends (and she probably was tempted to see it that way once in a while when things looked bleak), but Joy had the inner conviction that somehow this was part of God's design for her life now that Bill believed that their marriage should end.

Like her ancestor Abraham, Joy moved out on faith, taking one step at a time and living each day as it came. She learned from the outset of her adventure how ample was God's provision. After taking the train from Liverpool to London, Joy secured a room at the Avoca House Hotel, 43 Belsize Park, Hampstead, in northwest London. She chose this location because a number of writers, among them her pen friend, Phyllis Williams, lived in the neighborhood. Before Joy and the boys left New York, Bill had promised to pay child support of sixty dollars per week, and he assured Joy that her first check would be waiting at her friend's home when she arrived. However, after Joy checked in at Avoca House she was disappointed to learn that no money had been forwarded.

Booked into a hotel too expensive for her budget, Joy wanted to find rooms that she and the boys could afford. But two problems stood in her way. Bill had not come through with the promised money, and apartments were extremely scarce in London. Moreover, most refused to take children. Within five days, however, both problems were solved. Bill wired the first installment of child support; and when the owner of the hotel heard of her plight, she informed Joy that there was an apartment for rent in the hotel annex that she owned across the street. Furthermore, the flat was furnished, and children were welcome. The owner's policy was the result of her own difficulty in finding rental property allowing children when she had come to London from America in the 1930s.

Brimming with excitement, Joy described to Bill the ground-floor apartment: two large rooms complete with built-in mirrors, a grand piano tucked in one corner, and a door that opened onto a garden where the boys could play. Daily cleaning service was furnished, as were linens, towels, and utilities. Breakfast and dinner, "both large and good," were included for the total price of 12 guineas ($36) per week. Thankfully, she concluded that "The Lord really *is* my shepherd, by gum!"[15]

Douglas later remembered the Belsize Park apartment as a pleasant place. Joy took one room for her bedroom and sitting area, and the boys lived in the other. The toilet and bath were down the hall and shared by all tenants in the house. Near the gas heater was a small gas ring on the hearth, where Joy could fix a hot lunch and tea. Breakfast and dinner were served across the street at the hotel.[16]

Joy had no sooner settled the family into their new quarters than she began searching for a school. Good preparatory education, was expensive, but Joy was determined to place the boys in the best school she could possibly afford. After visiting several campuses, Joy selected Dane Court, which had been enthusiastically recommended by some writer acquaintances she had made. The school was located in Surrey, less than an hour's journey south from London. Joy's letters were full of enthusiasm about the boarding school, the quality of education, and how well the boys got on there. In later years, however, neither David nor Douglas had fond memories of the place.[17]

Whether the boys liked Dane Court or not was of little consequence to Joy Davidman. Because the quality of instruction was superior to that offered in the so-called ordinary schools, and because the boarding school was socially superior, Joy was confident that the cost of several hundred dollars a year was worth the sacrifice. As she told Bill in a letter designed to justify the expense, they had a responsibility to make "provision for the boys' future. As to what their careers will be, that's up to them; I only want them to have the kind of character and background that will fit them for what they choose."[18]

Once Joy found the best school they could afford, she acted on another high priority—visiting C. S. Lewis. Somehow she managed to wangle an invitation to spend four days at the Kilns in mid-December. After that interlude she told Bill that "both boys were a big success with the Lewises." The visit was peaceful, if strenuous. She recounted "long walks through the hills, during which Jack reverted completely to schoolboy tactics and went charging ahead with the boys through all the thorniest, muddiest, steepest places; Warnie and I meanwhile tailing behind and feeling very old." Warnie and Jack taught David chess, and "he astonished them by learning instantly and doing very well." Douglas won their hearts too, by "sawing huge armfuls of firewood, which was *very* well received."[19]

C. S. Lewis's version of the visit was similar to Joy's. He told one friend how he and Warnie entertained Joy and the boys for four days. "It went swimmingly," he said, "though it was very, very exhausting; the energy of the American small boy is astonishing." Lewis was clearly impressed by the precociousness of Douglas and David, observing that "without being in the least priggish, they struck us as being amazingly adult by our standards and one could talk to them as one would to 'grown-ups.' . . ." Jack was amused at how much they enjoyed open coal fires—especially the bellows that go with them. Their constant "look-out" for English policemen struck the Lewis brothers as humorous behavior as well.[20]

Douglas had vivid memories of this first meeting with C. S. Lewis, noting first of all that he found the man's looks most disappointing. Because Joy had told the boys so much about the great man at Oxford, Douglas found the first encounter to be a letdown. "Heroes were supposed to be dressed in a knight's armor," he said, "but this man looked so ordinary."[21]

Those first impressions soon passed, however, when Lewis insisted, somewhat to their mother's chagrin, that the boys call him Jack, and when he gave them a typescript of *The Horse and His Boy*, the fifth volume in the Narnia series, to take home and read. Added to their excitement was Lewis's promise to dedicate it "To David and Douglas Gresham," a wonderful gesture, making them feel loved and welcome despite being "strangers in a strange land."[22]

Joy felt good about the success of the trip and the renewal of her association with the Lewis brothers. She was wise enough not to overdo it though, recognizing "I shouldn't dream of visiting Jack often—we're much too exhausting an experience for that quiet bachelor household."[23]

The first year and a half in England was difficult for Joy in many ways. With the boys at Dane Court, she was lonely. She socialized now and then with science fiction writer Arthur Clarke, who had been a friend of both the Greshams some years earlier in the States. Joy saw Clarke and his wife at a Hampstead pub where many men and women writers congregated in the evenings. Joy also visited the boys in Surrey on Sundays after worshiping at St. Peter's Anglican Church near Avoca House, and spent an occasional evening with her writer friend Phyllis Williams.

C. S. Lewis visited London occasionally, but his schedule at Oxford and his writing projects did not allow frequent trips. He did try to put Joy in touch with some of his friends, hoping that she might strike up a friendship with a few of them. But many of Jack's friends found Joy brash, arrogant, and generally difficult. Only Jean Wakeman, a personable and highly intelligent writer who lived outside Oxford, and a few others, such as June and Roger Lancelyn Green and Austin and Katherine Farrer, befriended Joy. As the American author Sheldon Vanauken observed, Joy was misunderstood by English people. A personal style that might have gone unnoticed in New York was taken by the reticent British for deliberate abrasiveness.[24]

Joy's aggressive attitude and facial expressions, her sharp language, and love of argument for the challenge of it, were as natural to her as eating and breathing. She had been taught this behavior at her father's dinner table, and it was encouraged in her Columbia University seminars, and exacerbated by membership in the American Communist Party. What was seen as tough-minded but fair intellectual activity among Joy's New York acquaintances was viewed as rudeness and vulgarity in Lewis's Oxford circles. Nor did Joy's New York accent help her image among Lewis's friends. And the English tendency—at least among Lewis's companions— to keep women out of literary gab sessions served to make Joy's search for friends most difficult. Joy's status as a divorced, or about-to-be divorced, woman made things worse. No doubt her publication record made some people insecure. Her obviously brilliant mind, the breadth of her reading, and her nearly photographic memory intimidated still others.

Added to cultural differences and Joy's rather daunting intellect were some genuine shortcomings. Joy's bad temper surfaced from time to time, and she could be nastily censorious. She never suffered fools at all, and she caustically punctured sham and pomposity wherever she saw them. Joy had a tendency to view people in one of two ways: either they were her pupils and she lectured them, or they were her teachers and she pressed them hard for knowledge. As her brother remarked, Joy saw hardly anyone as equal.[25]

Joy also alienated many people by the certainty of her belief. If she was a true believer in Communist days, she was just as much so as a Christian. She viewed people who said "perhaps" and "maybe" with colossal contempt. Concomitant with her religious certainty and disdain for liberal fence sitting came an increasingly staunch conservatism. Indeed, Chad Walsh remembered that "she became a real Tory, lauding the merits of the gallows and the birch."

> The pain of aloneness was sometimes made more severe by poverty. There was never enough money to be comfortable, and Joy often skipped lunches when the boys were at school because finances were too sparse to allow her to buy the midday meal and still travel to Surrey on Sunday and take the boys out for a treat. Bill's promised support money seldom arrived on time. In fact, in an average year he sent only slightly more than half of what he had agreed to provide. It was not that he was indifferent to Joy's plight, but that he was having an increasingly hard time earning a living as a writer. Renée worked full time, but even with her

salary, she and Bill seldom stayed above the poverty line. Bill had to sell the farm at Staatsburg in order to pay back taxes, and eventually, he lost every dollar of equity to state and federal tax collectors.[26]

For Joy, the hardships of loneliness and penury could be mitigated by keeping busy. Desperately trying to earn money as a freelance writer, she pounded her typewriter day after day, often for ten or twelve hours at a stretch. By spring 1954 she had written several stories and one novel, but the novel never found a publisher and most of her stories met the same fate.[27]

"Courage was her shield," said one English friend, and it was nowhere more evident than in Joy's valiant attempts to earn money. She finally sold one nonfiction book outline entitled *Seven Deadly Virtues* to Hodder and Stoughton for one hundred pounds, and she did typing for Jack. Although she had offered to transcribe his manuscripts gratis, he insisted on paying; she knew he wanted to help her over the hurdles.

Joy also prepared an index for one of Warnie's books, and the publisher liked it so well that she was given several more to do. A job with a small magazine lasted until the periodical went bankrupt, and there were some royalties from Westminster for *Smoke on the Mountain*, which was published in the United States in November 1954; it was published in England by Hodder & Stoughton a few months later. In the year following publication, the American edition of *Smoke on the Mountain* sold about fifteen hundred copies. It sold over three thousand copies in Great Britain, probably because of Lewis's glowing foreword, which had been written too late for the American printing.[28]

Despite the royalties and some free-lance work, Joy could not earn enough to keep the household going. Regular employment was difficult to find in London under optimal circumstances, and

Joy's status as an alien made the situation impossible. Had it not been for the generosity of C. S. Lewis and her parents, it is hard to imagine how Joy would have survived the first year and a half. In spring 1954, and again in March 1955, Lewis helped pay the boys' tuition, room, and board. In August 1955 Joy wrote to Bill that "Jack was very pleased to hear you'd come through [with some money], but is insisting anyway on paying the school fees, and I can't afford to refuse. I hope it won't be necessary again."[29] But of course it was.

In October 1954 Joy's mother and father arrived in London. Jen and Joe informed their daughter that Renée's relationship with Bill was creating a split in the family. "It would appear," she wrote to Bill, "the Davidman family has been fighting over our affairs far more violently than we ever fought over them ourselves, and with that sublime disregard for truth and justice that characterizes the lot of them." With relief she celebrated that "I, at least, am safely on this side of the Atlantic; I hope Renée hasn't been having trouble." Magnanimously, Joy said, "When I can get a word in edgewise, I insist that at least a third of the responsibility for everything that happened is mine; you tell anyone I said so, if there's any occasion to."[30]

Joy's parents brought family gossip; they also brought presents and financial support. Joe and Jen bought their daughter a winter coat, and they purchased a bicycle for Doug's birthday. They stayed a few weeks in England, and then set out for a lengthy trip on the continent. In April 1955 they visited Joy and the boys on their way back to the United States. On the return portion of the journey they "replaced the boys' worn-out and outgrown clothes, thank Heaven, . . ." and they also treated Joy to some new clothing. Perhaps the greatest boon to Joy, she confided to Chad Walsh, was when they told her of their $25,000 in savings, and that if she and the boys became desperate, they would come to the rescue.[31]

During the elder Davidmans' sojourn in England, Joy introduced them to C. S. Lewis. "Jack had to come to London on the
27th [October 1954] to take part in a debate," Joy wrote, "and we
took him to tea at the Piccadilly Hotel beforehand. (His sugges-
tion; my organizing work; my parents' dough.)" Howard recalled
that Jen and Joe were quite favorably impressed with Lewis. They
were willing to overlook his credentials as an important Christian
apologist; the Davidmans were lifelong Anglophiles, and they
were proud that their daughter had been befriended by a brilliant
Oxford don who recently had been elected to a prestigious professorship at Cambridge University to begin the following term.[32]

Joy described tea at the Piccadilly to Bill, concluding that Lewis
"must be aiming for a halo" inasmuch as after tea he "invited us all
to lunch at Magdalen next week." Jack's invitation was awardwor-
thy because Jen and Joe were hard to endure at times:

> Jack laid himself out to be charming to both my parents
> and succeeded admirably; when I complimented him on it
> privately he said pathetically, "I'm doing my best!" Poor
> lamb; there were moments, as when my father lectured
> him on the blessings of Prohibition, when I saw his smile
> grow slightly fixed. I told the story of how, at age twelve, I
> priggishly poured Dad's private bottle of apricot brandy
> down the drain after hearing him proclaim his belief in Pro-
> hibition—and got myself walloped. Dad hadn't the sense to
> let it alone, but insisted that *his* was a special case, *he* wasn't
> really a breaker of the law, etc. This was too much for Jack,
> who remarked, "I think there was more than one prig in
> the family. Of course, our *own* case is always different isn't
> it?"[33]

Jen Davidman made a memorable first impression on Lewis,
too. Decked out in "a fancy black suit with rhinestone buttons, a

pearl bracelet, a pearl choker, dingle-dangle pearl earrings, a pink lace blouse and a shocking pink hat . . . I'll let you imagine Jack's reaction for yourself," Joy wrote.[34] Her own attire notwithstanding, Jen was appalled at the dress of one of the participants in the debate: Dorothy L. Sayers, whom Joy described as an "enormously witty and a very eloquent speaker, a forthright old lady who wears rather mannish clothes and doesn't give a damn about her hairdo." Jen's reaction was that "if brains made a woman look like that she was glad she wasn't intellectual."[35]

The Davidmans had not been back in America long when Joy's life took another turn. In August 1955 she and the boys moved to Headington, on the edge of Oxford, just one mile from the Lewis brothers at the Kilns. Ten, Old High Street was the address of the red brick dwelling where Joy and the boys resided. This Headington abode was half of a house—a duplex apartment—adorned with a rather large garden. When Joy, the boys, and a cat named Sambo arrived in August, there were ripe tomatoes on the vines, and plum and apple trees yielding fruit ready for picking.

To save train fare Joy, David, Douglas, and Sambo rode up to Oxford on the moving van with their belongings. The boys found this outing delightful; Joy merely liked the price. No sooner had they unpacked than Douglas purchased for ten shillings a budgerigar (Australian parakeet), complete with a cage, from an acquaintance in the neighborhood. David settled in and devoured books they purchased at Blackwell's, the "gigantic several-story bookshop in which you are encouraged to stay all day reading and not buying, if you like," as Joy put it.

Ten, Old High Street was, on a small scale, reminiscent of the farm. Joy cultivated flowers, herbs, and fruit; and she wasted no time in setting out tulip, iris, and daffodil bulbs. Within a few days another cat strolled in and was adopted. Before long Joy had acquired a mini-menagerie, which watched her as she picked plums and made jam.[36] Although much smaller than the old New York farmhouse, the semidetached red brick house on Old High Street was spacious in comparison to the London flat. Downstairs was a small kitchen, a separate dining room, and a parlor; the second floor held a bathroom and three bedrooms. The rent was significantly higher than what was charged at the Belsize Park address, but this was no problem. C. S. Lewis had located the house and encouraged Joy and the boys to move, and he paid the rent.[37]

Precisely what kind of relationship Jack and Joy had at this time is debatable. A number of Lewis's friends were, and still are, confident that Joy forced herself on Lewis, hounded him continually, and in essence became a nuisance. The only reason he befriended her, some say, was pity for her and the boys. This theory may have some basis in fact, especially if one considers the way Joy pursued a relationship with the Oxford bachelor in the early months after she moved to England. Joy initiated their first contact and did all in her strength to start a friendship and keep it alive.

Certainly Joy dreamed of marrying C. S. Lewis eventually. She mentioned this to her cousin, and she told her close friend from college days, Bel Kaufman, that she was deeply in love with Jack. But marriage was out of the question, despite the finality of Joy's divorce in August 1954. Lewis believed the official position of the Church of England made remarriage impossible. The Church maintained that marriage was indissoluble and therefore remarriage after divorce constituted adultery. But even if marriage seemed out of the question, Joy told Bel, the "most wonderful ecstasy came from just holding hands and walking on the heather."[38]

If the love in the relationship was one-sided in the beginning, it obviously did not stay that way long. Joy may have been clever enough to fool most people, but she was no brighter than Lewis;

and certainly no one could have duped him without awareness. Furthermore, he spent too much time with Joy to be seeing her merely out of a sense of duty or an expression of Christian charity. Perhaps he invited Joy and the boys to spend part of the summers of 1954 and 1955 at the Kilns simply because the acreage surrounding the house, and the woods and pond, were so good for two city waifs whose mother could not afford to take them on a proper holiday. Charity, if that is what it was, could have stopped there. Lewis's financial assistance, plus the offer of the Kilns for summer holidays, was clearly adequate to qualify for benevolence of the extra-mile variety.

Joy may have entrapped Jack into renting the house in Headington, where the boys were close enough to walk to the Kilns and swim everyday; perhaps she also pressured Lewis until he agreed to give David daily Latin lessons in August. Joy could not, however, have baited the strong-willed Lewis into walking to her house every day for a visit. Brother Warnie noted in his diary that once Joy moved to Headington, "she and J[ack] began to see each other every day. It was now obvious what was going to happen." But Jack denied anything of the sort. Jack, according to his brother, was "in her house every day, often stopping until eleven at night."[39]

One of the magnetic qualities that attracted Jack to Joy was the American's sense of humor. She had an uncanny ability to make the grown man bellow with boyish laughter—and this enchanted him. Douglas Gresham remembered a typical instance. It seems that Lewis had a fear of insects that went slightly beyond the ordinary. Joy recognized this and knew just how far to play it for fun. Once when Jack felt a small flying creature invade the hair on the back of his head, he frantically danced in place and called for Joy to "Get it out! Get it out!" As she inspected the invaded area and quietly removed the burrowing insect, she pretended to be unable to see it. Jack was nearly hysterical by the time she took mercy upon him and produced the captured culprit. At Joy's impish look, Jack laughed heartily.

While Jack Lewis may not have loved Joy at the beginning of their acquaintanceship, he most assuredly did so by summer 1955. Chad and Eva Walsh visited Joy and Jack in England that summer, and the perceptive Eva said she "smelled marriage in the air."[40] Warnie, too, recognized how close his brother and Joy were in 1955, and he analyzed the relationship this way: "For Jack the attraction was at first undoubtedly intellectual. Joy was the only woman whom he had met (although as his letters show, he had known with great affection many able women) who had a brain which matched his own in suppleness, in width of interest, and in analytical grasp, and above all in humour and sense of fun." Warnie saw that his brother brightened in Joy's company because "she shared his delight in argument for argument's sake, whether frivolous or serious, always good-humoured yet always meeting him trick for trick as he changed ground." Warnie likewise saw her as "A woman of great charity," yet one who displayed "unbounded contempt for the sentimental." Warnie applauded her ability to laugh at herself, especially when the high goals she set for herself led her into "seeming absurdities." Finally, Jack's brother came to love Joy like a sister, complimenting her by saying, "With all this, she was intensely feminine."[41]

When C. S. Lewis fell in love with Joy Davidman, her mind was certainly the initial attraction. When he described her soon after her death, he wrote: "Her mind was lithe and quick and muscular as a leopard. Passion, tenderness and pain were all equally unable to disarm it." Her intellect was manifested in a spirit that he found enthralling. "It scented the first whiff of cant or slush; then sprang, and knocked you over before you knew what was happening. How many bubbles of mine she pricked," he mused, and "I soon learned not to talk rot to her unless I did it for the sheer pleasure—and there's another red-hot jab—of being exposed and laughed at."[42]

She took one of those red-hot jabs at Jack after his inaugural address at Cambridge University in November 1954. Joy attended the event, which offered nearly "as much fuss . . . as a coronation." She "lurked modestly in the crowd," not bothering him because "he was walled about with caps and gowns and yards of recording apparatus." Lewis's lecture was "a great success," she believed, "but I think, for once, he was sacrificing accuracy in the interests of a good show."

Few people would have had the audacity—or the informed judgment—to take on Lewis. His thesis, as Joy heard it, was: "'old western culture' is quite dead, [and] has been supplanted by a machine-culture." According to Joy, Lewis continued, "We are now living in a 'post-Christian Europe' and learning about litera-ture from a representative of the older culture like himself is like learning about Neanderthal men *from* one or studying paleontol-ogy from a live dinosaur. . . . He ended," she said, "by telling them to study their dinosaur while they could, there wouldn't be any around much longer!" Joy claimed he "made a remarkably effec-tive case (with which I do not much agree) for the *really* important historic break between cultures," which she argued, came "not with the fall of Rome or the Renaissance but with the rise of sci-ence as power." The students "ate it up," she concluded, but she was going to have to challenge him.[43] Ultimately, they agreed to disagree.

More than just a stimulating challenger to Lewis, Joy became an asset. She likened herself to Scribners' Maxwell Perkins, the astute editor to whom the literary world was indebted for bring-ing out the best in F. Scott Fitzgerald, Alan Paton, Ernest Hem-ingway, Thomas Wolfe, and Ring Lardner. Joy had always worked with Bill in this way; never telling him what to write and certainly never censoring his work, she helped him formulate the ideas once they were created, and she was able to get his creative energy flowing when he hit periods of drought. In spring 1955 she offered to help Bill once again, after he had written complaining of writer's block. "Don't hesitate to consult me on any plot you're having trouble with, and we can maul it over all night by airmail!" Joy, in a bit of self-analysis, admitted, "I don't kid myself in these matters—whatever my talents as an independent writer, my *real* gift is as a sort of editor-collaborator like Max Perkins, and I'm happiest when I'm doing something like that."[44]

Joy began playing this role with Jack, and it was extremely important to him. Soon after he assumed the Cambridge professorship, he had more time on his hands than ever before. A professor, unlike a don, has far fewer demands on his time. But situated at Cambridge, in "a nice quiet room and all the time in the world," Joy wrote, "the inevitable has happened; he's dried up. He is quite worried about it. . . ."[45]

While Lewis was on break from Cambridge, he and Warnie invited Joy to visit. During this week at the Kilns she was writing, Warnie was writing, and Jack was mentally paralyzed. One night Jack "was lamenting that he couldn't get a good idea for a book" in writing. He and Joy settled into comfortable chairs, and "We kicked a few ideas around till one came to life. Then we had another whiskey each and bounced it back and forth between us." Joy was amazed that after this session "the next day, without further planning, he wrote the first chapter! I read it and made some criticisms (feels quite like old times)." Jack then "did it over and went on with the next. What I'd give to have his energy!"[46] Several weeks later Joy confessed that she could not "write one-tenth as well as Jack," but "I can tell him how to write more like himself! He is now about three-quarters of the way through his new book . . . and says he finds my advice indispensable."[47]

The book was *Till We Have Faces*. Published in 1956, it was dedicated "To Joy Davidman." Lewis's biographers, Walter Hooper and Roger Lancelyn Green, refer to it as "his greatest *tour de force*," and they go on to say that "to many readers, and probably to himself, [it is] his best work of fiction. . . . "[48] Humphrey Carpenter, author of *The Inklings*, agreed, and went even further. *Till We Have Faces*, he suggested, "is possibly Lewis's best book."[49] Some critics see Joy Davidman reflected in the novel's character, Orual. Carpenter theorizes Orual "may have been . . . in part a portrait of Joy. . . ." But he asks, "Was it not also a self-portrait of Lewis?" Carpenter quotes Lewis, who once said, "There ought spiritually to be a man in every woman and a woman in every man. . . ." In Orual, Lewis perhaps discovered his own entire nature. Like Orual who wore a veil to protect herself, Lewis's "manner, all his postures, had brought him success but had also, perhaps, hidden his inner nature not merely from others but from himself. It was only when his marriage somehow removed that veil," in Carpenter's opinion, "that he found his true nature."[50]

Jack had found in Joy something that stimulated—maybe completed—him. Like an adolescent boy, however, he was unsure just how to handle it. As brilliant and well educated as Lewis was, he was no man of the world. Not well traveled and rather inexperienced with women, he had settled into a predictable life living with his brother. Jack's image was one of an eccentric bachelor, and to break out of this mold was as uncomfortable for him as a teenage boy going from hating girls to being in love with one of them.

Hence, when Lewis fell in love, he was embarrassed to admit it. First of all, it was not what was expected of him. Secondly, the woman he happened to love was disliked by most of his friends. Some frowned on Joy because she was an American—an imposter—who was changing their world with C. S. Lewis. A few found Joy insufferable because of her explosive temper. George Sayer, for instance, recalled an incident that began during lunch with his wife, Moira, and C. S. Lewis one day in Oxford. Because George had business in town, he suggested that Moira go to the Kilns and read a book until he called for her, as they had often done. Jack seemed uncomfortable with the proposal but the Sayers thought little more about it until evening. While Moira was reading, Jack excused himself to take a nap. During his absence Joy walked in without knocking. She was whistling and carrying Jack's laundry. Upon seeing Moira she blurted out: "Who the hell are you, and what the bloody hell are you doing in this house?" Moira, who had met Joy earlier at one of Jack's luncheons, said, "We have met before and I have been invited here by Mr. Lewis." On that note Joy turned on her heel and left. Jack appeared from upstairs a little later, deeply saddened by what happened.[51] But he had brought it on himself because he had been unable, earlier in the day, to admit honestly his relationship to Joy.

Jack Lewis had another reason to be reticent about his relationship with Joy. Almost everyone knew her as Mrs. Gresham. Even after her divorce, she was Mrs. Gresham to most acquaintances. Divorce was not looked upon casually by people in Lewis's circle; there was a taint, a mark of shame, on someone who had discarded lifetime vows, regardless of the circumstances. To many, Christ's teaching was clear: divorced people could not remarry. To do so would be sinful. A divorced person who remarried committed adultery, and the new spouse was equally guilty.

Lewis himself did not take such a narrow view. He recognized that while Christianity teaches that the union of marriage should be a lifetime one, the views of different sects on divorce are quite diverse. Some forbid divorce; others allow it in special circumstances. In any case, Lewis frowned on divorce laws being forced upon everyone, finding the notion as appalling as prohibition laws.[52] However, if Lewis did not share the conservative position on divorce, his relationship with Joy was complicated by his role of spiritual mentor to many such conservative people. And some of his closest friends viewed remarriage after divorce as sin—utterly and emphatically.

Jack worried not only about friends, disciples, and the Church of England—there was also brother Warnie. The bachelor siblings had been together for years, neither having a spouse to compete with for attention or affection. Marriage would drastically change this long-standing relationship between Jack and Warnie. The thought of this must have given Jack great pause. Put succinctly, marriage to the woman he loved was going to be one of the most difficult decisions of his life.

As embarrassing as their relationship had become, however, their love for one another was good for both of them. Joy's letters after moving to Oxford and growing closer to Lewis reflect the calming effect he had on her disposition. The same serenity was evident in Jack. A lecturer at Oxford ran into Joy and Jack before they were married, one Sunday afternoon at Studley Priory, an Elizabethan-era private hotel north of Oxford. This place was a favorite of Joy's and Jack's, and they often stopped by on weekends to sip drinks and eat. Peter Bayley said Lewis "seemed very different: much more muted, gentle, and relaxed. Even his voice and laugh seemed quieter. I felt that his sensitive nature had at last come through a carapace of tough masculine clubbability."[53]

One very important reason for Joy's soothing effect on Jack was her ability to understand his mystical experiences. Until Joy happened along there was almost no one with whom he could talk about this part of his life, and fewer still who shared such experiences. J. R. R. Tolkien, for example, found preposterous Jack's mention of feeling Charles Williams's presence in his room one night after Williams died. To Tolkien, this was a subject unworthy of additional comment. Joy, on the other hand, could listen to Jack talk on such topics and seriously discuss the meaning of it all with him because she, too, had had similar visitations. She had perceived Christ's presence in New York on the eve of her conversion, and she had witnessed a wraith of Stephen Vincent Benét just after his death. At another time, long before she and Jack were married, she told him one morning she was haunted "with the obscure sense of God, (so to speak) 'at her elbow', demanding her attention." Lewis recalled the incident years later, pointing out that Joy, "not being a perfected saint . . . had the feeling that it would be a question, as it usually is, of some unrepented sin or tedious duty." But when Joy "gave in," wrote Lewis, "and I know how one puts it off—and faced Him, . . . the message was 'I want to give *you* something' and instantly she entered into joy."[54]

This encounter with "joy," told to Lewis before he finished writing his autobiography, plus Lewis's surprised involvement with this amazing woman named Joy, almost certainly endowed *Surprised by Joy* with a double, if not a triple meaning. He must have looked at her with a twinkle in his eye when he selected the title and forwarded it to the publisher.

These ties, as well as numerous other attractions, gave Lewis a genuine desire to marry Joy. Nevertheless, he might never have overcome his reluctance to face ridicule and censorship if external circumstances had not intervened. It is possible that Jack might have settled for holding hands while walking through the heather and chatting over tea at Studley Priory if the British Home Office, in early 1956, had not declined to renew Joy's permit to remain in England. Suddenly the Cambridge scholar faced the prospect of losing the company of the woman he loved. The thought of saying good-bye to Joy, of seeing the boys uprooted from school at Dane Court, and then knowing they all would be forced to go back to a tumultuous future in America, was more than Lewis could bear. He told George Sayer that he loved Joy, and he could not stand the thought of her "going back to that dreadful place"— meaning the United States in general, and New York with Bill and her parents in particular. Lewis made it clear to several others that he could not allow the boys to go back to America and the risk of being taken into custody by their father.[55]

It should be understood that by 1956 C. S. Lewis was not only in love with Joy Davidman, but loved Douglas and David as well. He felt protective of them; he felt responsible for their education and upbringing. Indeed, he was beginning to feel like their father. He most certainly empathized with them regarding their school experience. Neither David nor Douglas liked Dane Court, and Jack's heart ached for them because he could recall the misery he felt as a student at Malvern College.

Joy's correspondence makes it clear that Jack spent much time with the boys. When Douglas thought he couldn't survive without a football, Lewis bought him one. When David craved nothing so much as being turned loose in Blackwell's, Lewis took him and paid the bill. When David became interested in Greek, Lewis bought him a grammar and a Greek dictionary. Jack paid for the boys' schooling, clothing, and gifts; he bought them a horse and stabled it behind the Kilns.[56]

The prospect of giving up these loved ones forced Lewis to move quickly. On April 23, 1956, he and Joy were married in a civil ceremony at the Registry Office in Oxford. This act was as effective as the usual naturalization process. Being married to a British subject enabled Joy and the boys to remain in Britain for life. But Lewis was still reluctant to take on his critics and bring Joy into his life as a wife. Rather than seek permission from the Church of

England for a proper religious marriage, he pretended that this civil ceremony was nothing but a convenience—a way to keep Joy in England for her sake and the boys' benefit, rather than for his happiness as well. Jack told Warnie "that Joy would continue to occupy her own house as 'Mrs. Gresham,' and that the marriage was a pure formality designed to give Joy the right to go on living in England. . . ." But Warnie was not fooled.[57]

Only Kay and Austin Farrer, the Sayers, and a handful of others knew of the civil wedding. Jack was obviously not proud of this arrangement, and he did all he could to keep it a secret. Joy respected Lewis's feelings on this, never mentioning it in her letters to America until the status of the relationship changed several mouths later.

By fall 1956 gossip was growing about Jack's frequent visits to 10, Old High Street. When home from Cambridge he dropped in daily, often staying until late at night. Rather than allow Joy's reputation to continue to suffer, he began preparations for Joy and the boys to move into the Kilns.[58] Furthermore, he sought permission to marry in the Church of England. It was his argument that, inasmuch as Bill Gresham had been married and divorced before he married Joy, their union was no marriage in the eyes of the church. Consequently, on strictly legalistic grounds, there was no reason to deny them the sacrament.[59]

The Bishop of Oxford denied Lewis's request; but before Joy and the boys could move into the Kilns a crisis intervened, opening the way to an Anglican marriage. As early as June 1956, Joy complained about pain in her left hip. She told Bill "I've got fibrositis in one leg, my back, and my chest; which means I walk about all crippled up and it HURTS. The fault of the climate, of course; but I'm told it will pass."[60] Joy lived with the pain, typing a detective novel for Kay Farrer, who was trying to ease Joy's financial pinch. Joy was also doing some manuscript editing and pruning for Warnie.[61] Then the hammer dropped. In late October Joy fell; her hip gave out, and she couldn't walk. In excruciating pain she signaled a neighbor for help. She was rushed to the Wingfield Hospital, where it was discovered that she had cancer. The disease had eaten through her left femur, causing the weakened bone to break. The doctors also determined that she had a malignant lump in her breast.[62]

By early December, Joy was transferred to Churchill Hospital. Jack moved the boys into the Kilns, and he made preparations to announce his marriage to the world. Joy was urged to tell her friends and family in America that a wedding had taken place. Lewis placed an announcement in *The Times* on Christmas eve: "A marriage has taken place between Professor C. S. Lewis of Magdalene College Cambridge, and Mrs. Joy Gresham, now a patient in the Churchill Hospital, Oxford. It is requested that no letters be sent."[63] It was as if Jack wanted no shadow of shame cast on his Joy now, whatever the consequences to his pride and reputation.

As news spread about the marriage, friends and family also learned that Joy's condition was extremely critical—probably terminal. The doctors moved Joy back to Wingfield Hospital and gave her very little time to live and virtually no hope of recovery. Joy underwent three operations in November. The tumor was removed from her breast, but a mastectomy was not thought necessary. There was surgery to repair the broken femur, and then, as she phrased it, "they nipped out my ovaries as a precaution. . . ."[64]

Despite the bishop's refusal to bless their marriage, the constant pain in her hip, and the misery of continual vomiting from the effects of radiation treatment, Joy was usually able to soar above worldly troubles. Warnie was deeply moved by her witness, writing, "I never loved her more than since she was struck down;

her pluck and cheerfulness are beyond praise, and she talks of her disease and its fluctuations as if she was describing the experiences of a friend of hers."[65]

A letter she wrote to the Walshes reflected a deep spirituality and an ability to see good in the midst of this pain. Her "physical agony," she wrote, "was combined with a strange spiritual ecstasy. I think I know now how martyrs felt. All of this," she continued, "has strengthened my faith and brought me very close to God. . . ." Beyond these almost mystical feelings came an outpouring of thanksgiving. She was grateful for "Jack's love and care," and she told the Walshes, "You'll be glad to hear that I've made it up with my brother Howard, who's written very friendly and solicitous letters." She continued that "Warnie has been very good and the Lewis relatives are all writing from Ulster [Ireland], offering good wishes and vacation care for the boys—bless 'em." Finally, "Even my parents are at their best, offering any help I want. It's wonderful what a thing like this does for people!"[66]

Well into January 1957 Joy was peaceful, hopeful, and cheerful. Her attitude was remarkably positive. But by early February her mood changed; she fell into a pit of despair. She wasn't getting well, the radiation treatment seemed to have no effect, and her pain never took flight. She was showing neither signs of recovery nor imminent death. Her despair was poured out in a letter to her confidants in America:

> I am in rather a bad state of mind as yet—they had promised me definitely that the X-rays would work; I'd pinned all my hopes to having a year or so of happiness with Jack at least—and indeed it seems I shall lie about in the hospital with my broken femur waiting for death, and unable to do anything to make my last shreds of life useful or bearable.[67]

Joy went on to say "I am trying very hard to hold on to my faith, but I find it difficult; there seems such a gratuitous and merciless cruelty in this." She despairingly said, "I hope all we have believed is true. I dare not now hope for anything in *this* world."

Joy was not totally devastated, despite these cries from a disciple who was asking God, "Why?" A ray of optimism came at the end of the letter: "I fear all this will be horribly depressing for you; I shall go on praying for the grace to endure whatever I must endure, and perhaps I'll be more cheerful next time I write."[68]

Joy had rallied by the time she wrote to her friends a week later. She told the Walshes

> Everything looks much brighter than it did before. For one
> thing my prayer for grace has been answered. I feel now that
> I can bear, not too unhappily, whatever is to come, and the
> problem of pain just doesn't loom so large—I'm not at all
> sure I didn't deserve it after all, and I'm pretty sure that in
> some way I need it. . . . Jack pointed out to me that we were
> wrong in trying to accept utter hopelessness; uncertainty is
> what God has given us for a cross.[69]

During spring 1957, the forty-two-year-old cancer patient lay in the hospital praying for grace to accept her condition. This was all; she no longer prayed for healing. Warnie was praying for recovery; so was his brother. Jack even asked God to allow him to become Joy's substitute. He was willing to accept her pain, if it was God's will, just so Joy could be granted relief.[70]

C. S. Lewis also asked a friend, the Reverend Peter W. Bide, to come to Headington, lay hands on Joy, and pray for her recovery. A number of healings had followed Father Bide's previous ministrations, prompting Jack to request this friend and former student to intercede for Joy. Soon after his arrival at Headington, "the question of the marriage arose." Bide remembered that Lewis made the point that inasmuch as "Joy's first marriage had been to an already divorced man and therefore, in the eyes of the church, no such marriage was possible." Lewis and Bide both agreed that for the church to deny their request for marriage now was "to try to have your cake and eat it."

To Bide's mind, there was a further consideration of even more importance. "Joy desperately wanted to solemnize her marriage before God and to claim the grace of the sacrament before she died." Bide wrote: "It did not seem to me in the circumstances, possible to refuse her the outward and visible sign of grace which she so ardently desired and which might lead to a peaceful end to a fairly desperate situation."[71]

By March 21, Joy's case was diagnosed as hopeless. In Warren Lewis's words, "There seemed little left to hope but that there may be no pain at the end," and "Peter Bide consented to perform—a notable act of charity, for he is not of this Diocese, and had no right to do so without the Bp's [Bishop of Oxford] authority. However, at 11 a.m. we all gathered in Joy's room at the Wingfield—Bide, J., sister, and myself, communicated, and the marriage was celebrated."[72]

Soon after the vows were exchanged Joy was taken by ambulance to the Kilns to die. But sudden changes in her health were noticed. The pain disappeared from her hip at precisely the time Lewis began suffering from a bone disease that was diagnosed as osteoporosis. He told his friend and colleague Nevill Coghill "of having been allowed to accept her pain." Coghill inquired if he meant "that her pain left her, and that you felt it for her in your body?" Lewis replied "Yes, . . . in my legs. It was crippling. But it relieved hers."[73] Jack told his friend Sheldon Vanauken how intriguing it was that while he was suffering from a calcium deficiency in his bones (no reason was discovered for this problem),

"Joy who needed it [calcium] much more, was gaining it in hers. One dreams of a Charles Williams substitution! Well, never was gift more gladly given; but one must not be fanciful."[74]

Joy began to find relief from pain, and her general health began to improve. By May she was feeling stronger daily. Lewis wrote a hopeful but cautious note to a friend: "Forbidden and torturing hopes *will* intrude (on us both). In short, a dungeon is never harder to bear than when the door is opened and the sunshine and birdsongs float in."[75] Had Father Bide's prayers and laying on of the hands wrought a miracle? Were Warnie's, Jack's, and a host of other people's prayers being answered? Joy now began to pray for healing. More than anything else she wanted a normal marriage to Jack. Wherever she saw signs of hope, they were secretly, quietly, grasped.

Joy was saddened to have become a burden to Jack, draining his energy, and filling the Kilns with nurses, a sick bed, and two normally noisy boys that she could not corral. But Jack never complained. On the contrary, he saw the hand of God in this trial. Despite Joy's illness, he told a fellow believer, "You wd. be surprised (or perhaps you would not?) to know how much of a strange sort of happiness and even gaiety there is between us." [76] Jack told his friend Dom Bede Griffiths that "a new element of beauty as well as tragedy had entered my life. Certainly God has taken me at my word—I have for many years prayed 'Lord, take me out of myself, to seek and serve thee in others.' "[77]

In August 1957, Joy's dear friend Bel Kaufman arrived at the Kilns to see her presumably dying companion. Bel, by then an accomplished writer, had come bearing gifts and good wishes. She found Jack, according to her diary, "so much handsomer than his photos! Joy looks *wonderful*, though in bed, & knows [she] is fatally ill. Jack, too, has osteo-something, a degenerative disease—lack of calcium—back pains." Bel stayed for three days, talking to Joy and Jack, lunching at the Kilns on pheasant, and taking walks "on the moors in high wind. . . ." One afternoon the threesome had tea and played Scrabble, "in all languages."

On the morning of Bel's departure she "said good-bye to Joy as she went off in [an] ambulance for [radiation] treatment." Although they both knew they would not meet again this side of heaven, Bel found Joy to be beautifully serene and happy. "She was so peaceful and happy in that bed," Ms. Kaufman recalled, and one of the reasons for this was Joy's being so deeply in love. "In spite of the gravity of her illness," wrote Kaufman, "she said something to me that is memorable; it's a sentence I have even used in my own last book, *Love, Etc.* [Joy] said, referring to her marriage to Lewis: 'The movies and the poets are right: it does exist!'"[78]

Miracles were real, too. Less than a month after Bel Kaufman left the Kilns Jack wrote to a friend that Joy had surprised the doctors with her recovery. "My wife's condition . . . has improved, if not miraculously (but who knows?) at any rate wonderfully." Joy wrote four weeks later: "I am slowly learning to walk again—I can get about the house with a cane and two-inch lift on my shoe. This is little short of a miracle considering in April I was given two months at the outside, could not shift myself in the bed and had only broken fragments of a thigh bone!"[79]

Joy's progress continued to be remarkably good. By November she was walking about the house, riding in a car, and even going up and down a few steps. Running the household was her next goal, and perhaps writing after that. Jack celebrated the change, too, noting she could walk in the garden and get up to answer the telephone. Most encouraging, however, was the gradual disappearance of the diseased spots on her bones.[80] In January 1958, Joy's doctors shook their heads in bewilderment and pronounced her cancer arrested. Prayers of thanksgiving were offered up at the Kilns and in the houses of believing friends in England and America.

With almost boundless enthusiasm Joy began celebrating her reprieve and reveling in the freedom to be Jack's wife. Her own writing was given a low priority, although she did work from time to time on the manuscript of *Seven Deadly Virtues* and she concluded the research and outline for a biography of Madame de Maintenon, which Warnie had encouraged her to undertake. A top priority was assuring Warnie Lewis that she did not want to drive him from his own house. The major began preparations to move from the Kilns and set up housekeeping alone in Ireland. "But Jack and Joy would not hear of this," he wrote, "so I decided to give the new regime a trial." His fears about this marriage and his ability to live with brother and Joy in the same house were dispelled. "For me, Jack's marriage meant that our home was enriched and enlivened by the presence of a witty, broad-minded, well-read and tolerant Christian, whom I had rarely heard equalled as a conversationalist and whose company was a never-ending source of enjoyment. . . ."[81]

Joy did more than make Warnie feel a part of his own home; she tried to help him stop drinking. The major's friends and relatives all knew he had a severe problem with alcohol. His new sister-in-law attempted to help him by drawing upon her experience of alcoholism, acquired during her marriage to Bill Gresham.[82]

It was Jack and Warnie's habit, when they were both home, to spend the mornings writing and the afternoons answering correspondence. Jack got reams of letters from friends and admirers, and both Warnie and Joy helped him answer the flood of mail. Once while Jack was extremely busy, Joy wrote this letter to a friend named Mary:

Perhaps you won't mind a letter from me this time, instead
of Jack? He is having his first go at examining for the Cambridge tripos,* and is fairly drowning in examination
papers—apparently very silly ones! He comes up for air
now and then, blows a few pathetic bubbles, then sub-
merges again. He can't even get home for the next fortnight; our longest separation since our marriage, and we're
both feeling it badly!

I *am* sorry you've been having that nasty time in the
hospital. I know only too well what even the nicest hospital
is like; how the nurses all vanish at the one moment of the
day when you really need them, how the televisions and
wirelesses all around make night hideous, how the night
nurse wakes you from the first really refreshing sleep you've
had in a month, at midnight, to give you your sleeping pill.

. . . And you, I suppose, have been the subject of
demonstrations to medical students as well! In Oxford they
give students *their* examinations at some poor patient's bedside; examiners and students alike all done up in their mor-
tarboards and gowns, and scaring the patient half to death.
But I'm told that experienced patients have been known to
whisper the correct diagnosis to the student if he gets
stuck. . . .

Well, I hope you're home again now, and that it wasn't
too bad and they found the right answers. I can share too in
your thwarted desire to be useful. We women feel that
more than men, I think. There are a million things that
need doing around this house. Once I would have pitched
in and helped my housekeeper—but now, because I have to
walk with a stick and have only one hand free, I'm more

---

* The final honors examinations for the Bachelor of Arts degree.

nuisance than help and can only sit on the sidelines and give advice and be a pest. It *is* difficult having to accept all the time! But unless we did, how could others have the pleasure, and the spiritual growth, of giving? And—I don't know about you, but I was very proud; I liked the superior feeling of helping others, and for me it is much harder to receive than to give but, I think, much more blessed.

Then, too, it's only since I've been ill and helpless that I've realised just how good people in general are, when they have a chance. So many people have taken trouble over me, and have gone out of their way to give me pleasure or help! It's very heartwarming—and humbling, for I remember how cynical I used to be about humanity and feel a salutary shame.

Is your pet a cat or dog? I've found that cats stand these changes and separations pretty well—one of mine, when I was ill, took possession of a new home and mistress and had them completely under his thumb in a week. (If one can speak of a cat's thumb?)

Can you do any sort of hand work? I've found that making crocheted rugs and tablecloths, or knitting socks, was an amazing help with my spiritual difficulties when I was feeling low. One can work off so many frustrations by stabbing away with a knitting needle! It's better to make pretty things, I find, than just useful ones.

Of course we're both praying for you—and don't be too afraid, even if you turn out to need an operation. I've had three, and they were nothing like so bad as my fears.

> Blessings,
> Yours,
> Joy Lewis[83]

Joy always read Jack's manuscripts and served as his critic; she tried to aid Warnie in the same fashion. During 1958 she helped the major on *The Scandalous Regent* manuscript; when it was published, he dedicated it "To My Sister-in-Law JOY DAVIDMAN." In the acknowledgments to this volume of French history he wrote of his gratitude to Joy "for her kindness in reading my manuscript and for making many valuable suggestions."[84] Joy assisted Warnie with his work in French history, and she served as Jack's critic and editor for *Reflections on the Psalms* and *The Four Loves*.

And she did much more. Like a whirlwind, she set out to refurbish the Kilns. Jack and Warnie had lived there for nearly three decades and hardly anything had been done to redecorate, much less renovate. Joy wrote in February 1958: "Nothing had been done to [the Kilns] for about thirty years; the walls and floors are full of holes; the carpets are tattered rags—in fact," she assumed, only half-facetiously, that the house is "being held up by the books that line all the walls and if we ever move a bookcase All Fall Down! . . . I'm getting some cautious painting and repair done."[85] It cost a few pounds for Joy to carry out the overhaul, especially since she bought some new china and crystal to complement the elaborate meals she occasionally cooked. According to George Sayer she actually did not spend much money, but Lewis thought she did because he had seldom spent anything on the Kilns. Recognizing Jack's panic when he thought she might be overdoing it on expenses, Joy loved to come in and show him what she had bought, and then tell him the price. After he had nearly hyperventilated, she would laugh uproariously and tell him she got it on sale at half that total.

In truth, Joy saved Jack a lot of money. After moving into the Kilns she took over his checkbook, discovering thousands of pounds he did not even know he had. Furthermore, she encouraged him to take his small fortune out of a checking account and put it into a savings account and investments so that he could earn some interest on his capital.[86] Lewis was a notoriously poor manager of his own finances. Indeed, when he and Warnie were ready to purchase the Kilns back in 1930, the major discovered nearly nine hundred pounds in their account that Jack had entirely lost track of.[87] Clearly, there was a need for better record keeping and stewardship.

C. S. Lewis was not a wealthy man. He received but a modest salary from the university, and almost all of his royalties went into a charitable trust. Those funds underwrote numerous worthy causes, among them the educations of many seminarians, and Douglas and David Gresham's school expenses at Dane Court.[88] The advent of Joy, David, and Douglas cost Lewis some money. Not that Jack complained—he did not. However, Joy was pleased to be able to repay him, and probably with interest, by tidying up his accounts.

Once ensconced at the Kilns as Mrs. C. S. Lewis (she proudly used her new name on the return address portions of all correspondence), Joy was by no means wealthy, but she was more secure financially than she had been since she left her parents' protection in 1942 to marry Bill. Marriage to Jack freed Joy from monetary dependence on Bill Gresham, and she assured him "that I'd have to be pretty desperate before I took any legal action to collect what you owe me. I can only leave the matter to your own conscience."[89]

One matter, however, that Jack and Joy did not leave to Bill's conscience was the future of Douglas and David. When Bill learned that Joy was cancer ridden, with little hope of recovery, he wrote "naturally I shall want [Doug and Davy] to be with me in the event of your death."[90] Joy was petrified by this letter, and both boys expressed shock and anger. For the first time Jack intervened between Joy and Bill. Writing two letters to Bill on the same day (6 April 1957), Jack took his stand with force and clarity:

Joy is too ill to write and has asked me to answer yours of
the 2nd. This is a ticklish job. If through clumsiness, in the
effort to put things strongly, I sound like one who writes
with animosity, believe me this is not so. I think there has
never been any ill-feeling between you and me, and I very
much hope there never will be.

Your letter reached Joy after a day of agony. The effect
was devastating. She felt that the only earthly hope she now
has had been taken away. You have tortured one who was
already on the rack; heaped extra weights on one who is
being pressed to death. There is nothing she dreads so
much as a return of the boys to your charge. You perhaps
do not understand that certain scenes (when you were not
yourself) came early enough in their lives to make you a
figure of terror to them. Their return to the U.S.A. when
their education is finished is of course quite a different matter. Now, bitterly against their will, coming on top of the
most appalling tragedy that can happen to childhood (I was
through it and know), tearing them from all that has
already become familiar and shattering all sense of security
that remains to them, it would be disastrous. If you realized
the cruelty of what you are proposing to do, I am sure you
would not do it.

If you do not relent, I shall of course be obliged to
place every legal obstacle in your way. Joy has, legally, a
case. Her (documented) desire for naturalization (which
there may still be time to carry out), and the boys' horror
of going back, will be strong points. What is certain is that
a good deal of your money and mine will go into the
lawyers' hands. You have a chance to soothe, instead of
aggravating, the miseries of a woman you once loved. You
have a chance of recovering at some future date, instead of

alienating for ever, the love and respect of your children. For God's sake take it and yield to the deep wishes of everyone concerned except yourself.

You may suspect that a letter you will get from David was "inspired" by Joy or me. In reality, it was expurgated, i.e. the letter he meant to send was much stronger, and Joy made him tone it down. Douglas burst into tears on hearing your plans. I assure you that they have never heard a word against you from me. No *propaganda* at all has ever gone on.

Yours,

Jack

Dear Bill,

. . . What you and I have to think of is the happiness of the boys. I don't remember that Joy ever denied your *intention* to support them: she doubted, and doubts, your *power* to do so. That you have done all you *can* is important to any one who is making a judgment on your character (which of course I am not); but if what you can do is so little, the practical results will be the same for the boys won't they?

There is no question of your resigning yourself to "never seeing them again." Why should there not be a real, unconfused, reconciliation between you and them when they are grown up? But by forcing them back at a moment when their hearts are breaking, you will not facilitate this but render it permanently impossible. The boys remember you as a man who fired rifles throu' ceilings to relieve his temper, broke up chairs, wept in public, and broke a bottle over Douglas's head. David knew, and resented, the fact that you were living with your present wife while still married to his mother. Children have indelible memories of such things and they are (like us adults) self-righteous. . . .[91]

Bill had his share of shortcomings, but he did love his sons. He wanted them to be happy. As a consequence of these letters, he retreated from his request for the boys' return to America. When he visited David and Douglas, after Joy's death, he did not urge them to leave England and Jack and return with him to America.[92]

By 1959 Joy's health was on the upswing. There was no worry for the boys' future. The newlyweds were now free to celebrate life. Not all of their time was taken up with writing, editing, financial management, or redecorating. They talked, played Scrabble, and talked some more. They walked, went for drives in the country, read poetry aloud to each other, and sometimes cried from the depth of feelings they shared.[93]

In April 1958 Jack had written a friend:

Joy sends her love. We were away at a very nice country hotel last week having at last, what we never had before, a honeymoon! Here's another absurdity of the mind: I'm such a confirmed old bachelor that I couldn't help feeling I was being rather naughty ("Staying with a woman at a hotel!" Just like people in the newspapers!). I can't write more, for I'm travelling back to Cambridge to-day and the Vicar is coming in a few minutes to give Joy her Easter Communion (she still can't manage church).

God bless you more and more.

Yours,
Jack

P. S.—By the way, you are one of the *minority* of my numerous female correspondents who didn't gradually fade away as soon as they heard I was married.[94]

Jack summarized their marital relationship when he wrote in the journal which became a *A Grief Observed*: "She was my daughter and my mother, my pupil and my teacher, my subject and my sovereign; and always, holding all these in solution, my trusty comrade, friend, shipmate, fellow-soldier." He continued by labeling her "My mistress; but at the same time all that any man friend (and I have good ones) has ever been to me. Perhaps more." Lewis observed, "If we had never fallen in love we should have none the less always been together, and created a scandal."[95]

Jack now seemed oblivious, or indifferent, to the fact that they *had* created a scandal. Before they were married, after the bedside service—and even today, many Lewis disciples are embarrassed by his relationship with Joy Davidman. But Jack overcame his childish red-facedness about their love affair once she moved into the Kilns and was granted more time to live. Unashamedly he told the world in *The Four Loves*, published in 1960: "Years ago when I wrote about medieval love-poetry and described its strange, half make-believe, 'religion of love,' I was blind enough to treat this as an almost purely literary phenomenon, I know better now." He told several people, in essence, what he wrote to a friend: "It's funny having at 59 the sort of happiness most men have in their twenties . . . [ellipses his] 'Thou has[t] kept the good wine till now.'"[96]

They shared the good wine in travel, going to Solva, Wales, for a seaside holiday. Although neither of them had flown before, they took an airplane to Ireland. Jack escorted his bride around the land of his birth, showing her the haunts of his youth, introducing her to relatives and to his close friend of many years, Arthur Greeves. She loved his Ireland, waxing eloquent in describing it to Bill:

> We had a heavenly time; beautiful sunny weather, miracu-
> lous golden light over everything, clear air in which the
> mountains glowed like jewels—there isn't a speck of dust
> in the whole country. We drove about in a leisurely way
> through the Carlingford Mountains, the Mourne Mountains
> (*not* the mountains of "Mora," but they do sweep down to
> the sea) and finally Donegal. The country is all rocks—
> granite hillsides like the roughest of New England, and dry
> stone walls everywhere—and completely lacks the lush gar-
> den quality of England; there's a good deal of austerity in
> its beauty, but it is the most beautiful place I've ever seen.[97]

The summer of 1959 had been a glorious one for the Lewises. They took in the Welsh seaside, Ireland, and the English country-side. By autumn Joy could walk a mile at a time without growing overly exhausted. She could even wander through the woods at the Kilns once again, chasing away trespassers with a shotgun— once again leaving Jack's friends aghast by her "crude" behavior.

When the holiday season was over and Jack had started a new term at Cambridge, Joy praised God for her strength and health. "I stay miraculously well and active," she wrote, "my last X-rays showed a few holes here and there in my bones that won't quite vanish, but at least they don't grow."[98]

The plucky woman who now walked everywhere with a cane, and who had put on considerable weight since her radiation ther-apy began, had only one complaint by fall: "I *do* have a lot of pain, on and off, with rheumatism and strained muscles—it's not easy walking about with one thigh more than three inches shorter than the other—" but no mind, she signed off, "I'm assured these aches don't mean a thing. . . ."[99]

The aches meant more than the doctors realized. The next month, almost precisely two years after the healing was diagnosed, the dreaded cancer reappeared. Jack had told more than one confidant that they lived with "the sword of Damocles over us."[100] In October 1959 it fell.

As Jack recounted in a letter to America:

> Will you redouble your prayers for us? Apparently the wonderful recovery Joy made in 1957 was only a reprieve, not a pardon. The last x-ray check reveals cancerous spots returning in many of her bones. There seems to be some hope of a few years of life still and there are still things the doctors can do. But they are all in the nature of "rear-guard actions." We are in retreat. The tide has turned. Of course God can do again what He did before. The sky is not now so dark as it was when I married her in hospital. Her courage is wonderful and she gives me more support than I can give her.
>
> The dreadful thing, as you know, is the waking each morning—the moment at which it all flows back on one.[101]

By December Joy was holding her own. "I'm not as well as I was," she told Bill, "a few new spots in my bones and lumps here and there—but so far they melt away beautifully before X-rays."[102] The waves of radiation did not conquer the enemy this time. In March she confessed that while she was still on her feet, "and not in more pain than codeine can control, . . . I've got so many cancers at work on me that I expect them to start organizing a union." Joy admitted that she was losing ground, but at least the cancer gained on her "very slowly."[103]

The savage spread of the disease notwithstanding, Joy and Jack determined to recapture the magic of the previous summer and take one more trip. Both of them yearned to see Greece, a land of history and culture that had generated a language and literature they both admired. Not daring to wait until summer, they went in April, accompanied by their friends June and Roger Lancelyn Green, for a twelve-day visit. They had a glorious time. Lewis wrote later that month:

> We did get to Greece, and it was a wonderful success. Joy performed prodigies, climbing to the top of the Acropolis and getting as far as the Lion gate of Mycenae. She has (no wonder) come back very exhausted and full of aches. But I would not have had her denied it. The condemned man is allowed his favourite breakfast even if it is indigestible. She was absolutely enraptured by what she saw. But pray for us: the sky grows very dark.
>
> I can't begin to describe Greece. Attica is hauntingly beautiful and Rhodes is an earthly paradise—all orange and lemon orchards and wild flowers and vines and olives, and the mountains of Asia on the horizon. And lovely, cheap wine. I've eaten squid and octopus! [104]

Three years later C. S. Lewis still remembered this as a special time in their lives and told Walter Hooper: "Joy knew she was dying, I knew she was dying, and *she* knew I knew she was dying—but when we heard the shepherds playing their flutes in the hills it seemed to make no difference!"[105]

Joy would have been willing to meet death on this trip; she probably wished for it. In a letter written a week before their flight to Athens she acknowledged that going on such a trip is "a big chance in my condition, but the doctors say OK and I'd rather go out with a bang than a whimper . . . particularly on the steps of the Parthenon!"[106] But there was no dramatic death scene anywhere in Greece. Joy returned home to several weeks of pain and nausea. On May 20 she was taken to the hospital for more surgery. Her right breast was removed.[107]

In early June she was back at the Kilns in excellent spirits, but without signs of remission. She and Jack talked and played Scrabble, and Warnie pushed her in a wheelchair through the gardens and out to the pond. Continually thinking of others, she managed to purchase a dozen handkerchiefs for Warnie's sixty-fifth birthday on June 16. She was also able to write letters to Bill, who was planning a visit to Oxford in early August, and tell him what to bring in the way of necessities and what to expect from his teenaged sons.[108] In the midst of helping Bill plan for his first trip to England, Joy fell desperately ill and was hurried to Acland Hospital. On June 21 Warnie wrote in his diary "Joy is dying in the Acland." David and Douglas were brought home from school to be with their mother during her last hours.[109]

Once again, Joy astounded Jack, Warnie, nurses, and doctors. Within a week she was home. Although there was some pain and occasional vomiting, she was well enough to sit up, play Scrabble, and carry on conversations with Jack; but as Warnie observed, "it cannot be more than a reprieve."[110]

The respite was brief. Four days after getting home from the hospital Joy and Jack had their Sunday lunch at Studley Priory, and on Monday Joy was taken for a drive in the Cotswolds. Later in the week she was in considerable pain, yet perfectly lucid and able to sit up. She and Jack both knew the end was very near, and once during this time Jack said: "If you can—if it's allowed—come to me when I too am on my death bed." "Allowed!" retorted Joy.

"Heaven would have a job to hold me; and as for Hell, I'd break it into bits." As Jack pointed out, "She knew she was speaking a kind of mythological language, with even an element of comedy in it." He said, "There was a twinkle as well as a tear in her eye. But there was no myth or joke about the will, deeper than any feeling, that flashed through her."[111]

On Tuesday night, July 12, Warnie went off to bed. When he bade Jack and Joy good night, Joy looked "remarkably better" and "felt much more comfortable." She and Jack were playing Scrabble and chatting. As Warnie "dropped off to sleep they sounded as if they were reading a play together."[112]

At 6:15 the next morning Warnie awakened to Joy screaming—something she never did. The strong woman who had always taken pain gracefully was writhing in agony. Jack went with her to the Radcliffe Infirmary. She did not lose consciousness during her last hours, but dozed from time to time. During an alert period in the afternoon, Joy asked Jack to give her fur coat to Kay Farrer and expressed her wish to be cremated. Joy also asked their friend, Austin Farrer, an ordained Anglican priest, to preside at her funeral. One last wish, she told Jack, was "Don't get me a posh coffin; posh coffins are all rot."[113]

Later that night she received absolution from Austin Farrer. At 11:20 P.M. she told him, "I am at peace with God." Then Jack witnessed her last smile, but it was not for him or Austin.[114]

Chapter 5

LEGACY

"In Ashes, Yet with Hope. . . ."

J oy's funeral was held Monday morning, July 18. Jack, Warnie, David, and Douglas climbed into one taxi; Joy's nurse and the housekeeper family, Mollie and Len Miller, followed in a second car.

As the two cars of mourners entered the roundabout on the way to the funeral, the hearse carrying Joy's simple coffin and remains pulled into the intersection ahead of them. "We fell in behind the hearse," Warnie noted, "by chance, not design . . . and for last time poor dear Joy drove out along the road to Studley."[1]

It was a special day of the kind that tempts one to think God arranged the weather to symbolize the child who had joined Him. The sunny morning, with large white clouds in the sky, warned of possible storms. There was wind, too—the sort of day that exudes power rather than tranquility.[2]

Although Joy died at peace and there was a calmness emanating from her throughout the painful illness, her life had been far from serene. Once she began a relationship with Jesus Christ, there was a sunny quality about her personality, but storm clouds were always in the background. They sometimes passed over; but occasionally they erupted into outbursts of temper or in crises that beset the embattled pilgrim. And finally, her entire adult life manifested intellectual, verbal, and eventually spiritual power. Strength rather than placidity characterized Joy's personality.

The service was held at the Headington Crematorium in a plain, sunlit chapel, with Austin Farrer presiding. Warnie noted in his diary that Austin had difficulty reading the service because of the "great emotional strain," a problem compounded by the fact that "none of J[ack]'s friends bothered to put in [an] appearance." At the close of the service the casket was silently rolled away, "and curtains, pulled invisibly, hid it from us for ever."[3]

Sometime after Joy's cremation Jack composed a brief verse in her memory. It was inscribed on an austere marble plaque shaped like a crucifix, and mounted on a memorial wall in the crematorium garden. The inscription reads:

Remember

Helen Joy

Davidman

D. July 1960

Loved wife of

C. S. Lewis

Here the whole world (stars, water, air,

And field, and forest, as they were

Reflected in a single mind)

Like cast off clothes was left behind

In ashes yet with hope that she,

Re-born from holy poverty,

In lenten lands, hereafter may

Resume them on her Easter Day.

Joy Davidman's cancer-riddled body was now ashes and dust, but Jack and Warnie were comforted by their belief in everlasting life for all believers. Joy had expressed her own faith in eternal life to one correspondent when she wrote, "I believe in some kind of life after death (without being specific as to its nature)." And she quoted her oneness with Saint Paul on the issue, writing that the apostle "faced this issue squarely; when asked, 'What if you Christians are wrong about the afterlife?'" With Paul, she said no people could be more wretched than Christians if they are wrong about this doctrine. For if there is not a life with Christ beyond this world, then the only good things are in and of this world—and Christians are called to give up these things while they are building a new Jerusalem.[4]

On separate occasions Warnie and Jack each experienced what was, to them, confirmation of Joy's ongoing life. On the day of the funeral, Warnie wrote, "At times during the morning I felt Joy very close to me."[5] Jack noted in *A Grief Observed*, "even if I got what seemed like an assurance of [Joy's] presence, I wouldn't believe it." However, after such an encounter Lewis admitted that refusing to believe it is

Easier said than done. Even now, though, I won't treat anything of that sort as evidence. It's the *quality* of last night's experience—not what it proves but what it was—that makes it worth putting down. It was quite incredibly unemotional. Just the impression of her *mind* momentarily racing my own. Mind, not "soul" as we tend to think of soul. Certainly the reverse of what is called "soulful." Not at all like a rapturous re-union of lovers. Much more like getting a telephone call or a wire from her about some practical arrangement. Not that there was any "message"—

just intelligence and attention. No sense of joy or sorrow.
No love even, in our ordinary sense. No un-love. I had
never in any mood imagined the dead as being so—well, so
business-like. Yet there is an extreme and cheerful intimacy.
An intimacy that had not passed through the senses or the
emotions at all.[6]

Regardless of what we believe about visitations from those
who have departed this life, Joy does live on in other ways to everyone left behind. C. S. Lewis was every bit as much *"inspired* by Joy"
as he was "surprised" by her. *A Grief Observed* is as much her legacy of comfort to those who have lost loved ones as it is a gift from
Lewis himself. And it is a good guess that he would be the first to
acknowledge this.

Joy's indelible imprint continues in several other books written
by her husband. *Reflections on the Psalms* (1958) was his first book
on faith, aside from his spiritual autobiography, edited volumes of
addresses, and allegories for children, since *Miracles*, published in
1947. Humphrey Carpenter convincingly argues that Lewis was so
devastated by an attack on *Miracles* by an able Christian, Elizabeth
Anscombe, that he avoided writing Christian apologetics for a
decade.[7]

Lewis's relationship with Joy brought him out of hiding. Joy's
enthusiasm for her newly acquired faith and her admitted deter-
mination to use her writing gifts to defend and promulgate Christianity conspired to goad Lewis on. When Joy called upon him to
offer criticism on her manuscript, *Smoke On the Mountain: An Interpretation of the Ten Commandments*, he did so, complete with a foreword to the English edition as well.

Delving into Christian apologetics once again became a tonic
to Lewis. Soon after helping Joy on her book, she encouraged him
to write the volume on the Psalms he had contemplated ten years

earlier. This he did, and as Roger Lancelyn Green and Walter Hooper noted, Joy, with her Jewish background, proved a help and an inspiration.[8]

Joy's legacy survives in other books, especially *Till We Have Faces* (1956, 1957) and *The Four Loves* (1960). Little touches from Joy are apparent in the last volume of the Chronicles of Narnia, *The Last Battle* (1956), where for example, Tirian, refers to Jill as "comrade." "Comrade" was not a natural form of address to Lewis. Joy, on the other hand, because of her early Communist Party affiliation, used the term often. Evidently the habit touched Lewis.

Joy left scores of poems and her novel *Anya* to posterity. Although they do not reflect her mature spirituality, these works are significant contributions to American letters. Her second novel, *Weeping Bay*, carries a powerful spiritual message, and it will continue to inspire people who are fortunate enough to find a rare copy.

Smoke on the Mountain is still in print three decades after the first edition was published. Joy's first attempt at a book of nonfiction, this compact volume is a unique interpretation of the Ten Commandments by a Jewish Christian. Joy Davidman the prophetess lives in this volume, and her call to obedience, and admonitions to turn from worldliness are as refreshingly crisp now as they were when originally published. A magnetic theme of the book is the beckoning to a "joyous Christianity." Joy maintains that obeying God will make us happy; through obedience to God's commandments we experience joy and better understand His love for us.[9]

Perhaps Joy's greatest legacy is the example of her transformed life. For over thirty years she walked the way of self-indulgence and atheism. Then she turned abruptly around and followed the beckoning of Jesus Christ. If her walk with Him was frequently graceless and faltering, it was also committed, courageous, and faithful.

AFTERWORD

Within three years after Joy's death, two of the important people in her life died, too. Bill Gresham passed away in New York City in September 1962. He had cancer. C. S. Lewis died at the Kilns in November 1963. He was never well after Joy left him.

Prior to Lewis's death, David Gresham moved away to continue his education. He now lives in Europe. Douglas Gresham lived with Joy's close friend, Jean Wakeman, after C. S. Lewis died. He now presides over four farms in Tasmania, Australia, with his wife Merrie and their four children.

Major Warren Hamilton Lewis departed this life in 1973 at the Kilns. He was two months short of his seventy-eighth birthday.

Renée Gresham basks in the warm climate of Gulf Coast Florida. Her home is at Port Charlotte where her daughter, Rose Mary Simmons, lives with her husband Jack and their two children. Renée's son, Bob Pierce, lives in New York.

Howard Davidman maintains a private practice as a psychiatrist in New York City.

⁓

February 2009

More than a quarter century has passed since I wrote this biography of Joy Davidman. Because so many people over the years have written and told me how much Joy's story encouraged them, I am extremely grateful to Patricia S. Klein and her colleagues at

Hendrickson Publishers for bringing out this new edition of Joy's story.

Much has changed since I wrote the Afterword to the original edition of *And God Came In*. Both Renée Gresham and Howard Davidman have passed away, and Douglas and David Gresham moved to new homes and involved themselves in many worthy enterprises.

The questions I am most frequently asked about Joy and C.S. Lewis are these: What do you think about the two *Shadowlands* films, and what do you make of the numerous biographies of C. S. Lewis? Regarding the first question, I always answer that the second movie, starring Debra Winger as Joy and Anthony Hopkins as Jack, is by far the best. Debra Winger played Joy quite well given the script she was given. Likewise it is astounding how much Ms. Winger looks like Joy when she and Jack first met. Nevertheless, everyone who sees this film, or the first one for that matter, should keep in mind that these movies are fiction. Not only were many significant facts about the lives of the Lewises altered, several fictional scenes were added for dramatic effect. This is unfortunate inasmuch as the real story is much more interesting and powerful and it certainly gives more glory to God.

The question about biographies of Lewis is more complicated. By far the best biography of Lewis is the one written by his long-time friend George Sayer. Titled *Jack: C.S. Lewis and His Times* (1988), this is still the nearest thing to a definitive biography of Lewis that we have. There are some other useful biographies available but I must warn readers that the one by A.N. Wilson is a dreadfully inaccurate and deliberately misleading book. In contradistinction to Wilson's volume are two books by Douglas Gresham, *Lenten Lands: My Childhood with Joy Davidman and C.S. Lewis* (1988) and *Jack's Life* (2005). These two books stand out because Douglas has personal insights no one else can offer. Finally I wrote *Seeking the Secret Place: the Spiritual Formation of C.S. Lewis* (2004) to bring light to this overlooked dimension of Lewis's life.

Readers who want to learn more about the personal lives of C.S. Lewis and Joy Davidman would profit from examining the library and archives of the Marion E. Wade Center, Wheaton College, Wheaton, Illinois. The Wade Center's massive collection of letters written by both C.S. Lewis and Joy Davidman, as well as the C.S. Lewis Oral History Collection, comprise the richest library of Lewisiana in the world.

NOTES

The following abbreviations are used in the Notes:

HD: Howard Davidman
JD: Joy Davidman
LD: Lyle Dorsett
DG: Douglas Gresham
RG: Renée Gresham
WLG: William Lindsay Gresham

All of the Joy Davidman and William Lindsay Gresham correspondence is in the Marion E. Wade Collection, Wheaton College, Wheaton, Illinois, except for Joy's letters to Chad and Eva Walsh and Kenneth Porter. Originals or copies of the letters to the Walshes and Porter are owned by Dr. Chad Walsh, Lake Iroquois, Vermont.

Chapter 1

1. Joy Davidman. "The Longest Way Round," in David Wesley Soper, ed., *These Found the Way: Thirteen Converts to Protestant Christianity* (Philadelphia: Westminster Press, 1951), p. 13.
2. Ibid.
3. Moses Rischin. *The Promised City: New York's Jews*, 1870–1914 (New York: Harper & Row, 1970), p. 94.
4. Interview with Renée Gresham, Port Charlotte, Florida, May 26–28, 1981, and January 21–23, 1982, hereafter cited as RG to LD. Interview with Howard Davidman, New York City, July 21–22, 1981, hereafter cited as HD to LD. Copy of a letter from William Lindsay Gresham to David Gresham, June 26, 1962, William Lindsay Gresham Papers, Wheaton College, Wheaton,

Illinois; hereafter Gresham's correspondence in this collection will be cited WLG.

5. Nathan Glazer, "Jewish Loyalties," *Wilson Quarterly*, Vol. 5, no. 4 (Autumn 1981), p. 142.

6. HD to LD.

7. Thomas Kessner, *The Golden Door: Italian and Jewish Immigrant Mobility in New York City*, 1880–1915 (New York: Oxford University Press, 1977), pp. 154–55 contain useful material on Jewish mobility.

8. Oliver Pilat, "Girl Communist," *New York Post*, October 31– November 13, 1949. See also Irving Howe, *World of Our Fathers* (New York: Simon & Schuster, 1976), p. 214.

9. HD to LD.

10. RG to LD; HD to LD.

11. HD to LD.

12. HD to LD.

13. Douglas Gresham to LD, interview June 2–5, 23–25, 1982, Boulder, Colorado; and Wheaton, Illinois. Hereafter cited DG to LD. Quotation comes from David Gresham to LD, November 13, 1981.

14. RG to LD; HD to LD.

15. HD to LD.

16. HD to LD.

17. HD to LD.

18. HD to LD.

19. RG to LD.

20. Davidman, "The Longest Way Round," p. 15.

21. Mary Ellen Gresham to Dr. Clyde Kilby, November 11, 1973, Joy Davidman File, Marion E. Wade Collection, Wheaton College, Wheaton, Illinois. Howard Davidman told me how his parents feared to travel outside the Northeast.

22. Pilat, "Girl Communist."

23. HD to LD.

24. Pilat, "Girl Communist."

25. Davidman, "The Longest Way Round," p. 13.

26. Ibid., p. 16.

27. Ibid.

28. Ibid.

29. Ibid.

30. Ibid., pp. 17–18.

31. Ibid., p. 17.

32. Pilat, "Girl Communist."

33. Board of Education, *A Long-Range Plan for the City of New York* (New York: Board of Higher Education, 1962), pp. 1, 66, 282.

34. Telephone interview with Bel Kaufman, December 22, 1981. Bel Kaufman to LD, December 5, 1981.

35. *Wistarion* (New York: Schilling Press, 1934), Vol. 32, 1934; Bel Kaufman to LD, December 22, 1981; HG to LD. *Wistarion* is the Hunter College Yearbook.

36. Bel Kaufman to LD, December 22, 1981; HD to LD.

Chapter 2

1. Oliver Pilat, "Girl Communist," *New York Post*. October 31– November 13, 1949.

2. Transcript for Helen Joy Davidman, Columbia University Transcript Records; Pilat, "Girl Communist."

3. HD to LD.

4. Abraham Poneman to LD, March 8, 1982.

5. Pilat, "Girl Communist."

6. Ibid.

7. *Poetry*, Vol. 47 (January 1936), p. 193; Vol. 49 (March 1937), p. 323.

8. HD to LD.

9. Charles A. Fenton, *Stephen Vincent Benét* (New Haven: Yale University Press, 1960), reprint ed. (Westport, Conn.: Greenwood Press, 1978), pp. 263–64.

10. Stephen Vincent Benét, Foreword to Joy Davidman, *Letter to a Comrade* (New Haven: Yale University Press, 1938).

11. *Books*, December 25, 1938, p. 2; *The New York Times*, August 6, 1939, p. 4; *Poetry*, Vol. 54 (April 1939), p. 33. All of these reviews are cited in *Book Review Digest*, 1939, p. 232.

12. All of the quotations are from *Letter to a Comrade* (New Haven: Yale University Press, 1938), 2d printing, April 1939.

13. Benét, Foreword to *Letter to a Comrade*.

14. Charles A. Fenton, ed., *Selected Letters of Stephen Vincent Benét* (New Haven: Yale University Press, 1960), p. 340.

15. The MacDowell Colony records show that Joy was there in 1938, 1940, 1941, 1942. *New Hampshire: A Guide to the Granite State*, American Guide Series (Boston: Houghton Mifflin, 1938), pp. 218–21, gives an excellent history and description of the town and colony at the time Joy was there. Some useful data was also gleaned from the brochures supplied to me by the MacDowell Colony.

16. HD to LD.

17. Joy Davidman, *Anya* (New York: Macmillan, 1940). On p. 72 is the quotation "no man . . . " Examples of the sensuousness of *Anya* are numerous. See, for example, pp. 26, 41, 67, 81, 129, 188, 267. The reference to D. H. Lawrence is on the inside flap of the dust jacket.

18. Ibid., p. 67.

19. Ibid., p. 87.

20. The reviews quoted appeared in *Books*, July 14, 1940, p. 2; *The New York Times*, July 14, 1940, p. 7; and *Saturday Review of*

Literature, July 13, 1940, p. 10. All of these reviews are cited in *Book Review Digest*, 1940, p. 226.

21. Pilat, "Girl Communist."

22. For good background on the Communist Party see Richard Pells, *Radical Visions and American Dreams* (New York: Harper & Row, 1973), and Maurice Isserman, *Which Side Were You On? The American Communist Party During the Second World War* (Middletown, Conn.: Wesleyan University Press, 1982).

23. Joy Davidman, "The Longest Way Round," in David Wesley Soper, ed., *These Found the Way: Thirteen Converts to Protestant Christianity* (Philadelphia: Westminster Press, 1951), p. 19.

24. Pilat, "Girl Communist."

25. Davidman, "The Longest Way Round," p. 19.

26. Ibid., pp. 19–20.

27. Pilat, "Girl Communist."

28. Ibid.

29. Ibid.

30. Davidman, "The Longest Way Round," pp. 20–21.

31. Ibid., p. 21.

32. JD to Kenneth Porter, March 31, 1939. Copies lent to me through the courtesy of Dr. Chad Walsh, Lake Iroquois, Vermont.

33. Ibid.

34. JD to Kenneth Porter, February 19, 1939.

35. Pilat, "Girl Communist."

36. HD to LD.

37. Her rationalization for not returning to Hollywood is quoted in Pilat, "Girl Communist."

38. Fenton, *Benét*, pp. 233–40.

39. Nina Schneider to LD, November 30, 1981. Joy signed off her letters "comradely" and in Russian to Kenneth Porter. See JD to Kenneth Porter.

40. Quoted in Larry Ceplair and Steven Englund, *The Inquisition in Hollywood: Politics in the Film Industry*, 1930–1960 (Garden City, N.Y.: Anchor Press/Doubleday, 1980), quoted on p. 56.

41. Ibid., pp. 56–57.

42. Franklin Folsom to LD, May 31, 1982.

43. Pilat, "Girl Communist."

44. Ibid.

45. *New Masses*, June 10, 1941, pp. 12, 13; and Pilat, "Girl Communist."

46. JD to Kenneth Porter, March 31, 1939.

47. Mary Ellen Gresham to Dr. Clyde Kilby, September 26, 1973. Joy Davidman File, Marion E. Wade Collection, Wheaton College, Wheaton, Illinois.

48. Jerome Hoffman to LD, February 14, 1982.

49. Ibid.

50. HD to LD.

51. *New Masses*, March 29, 1941; April 1, 1941.

52. *New Masses*, April 14, 1942.

53. *New Masses*, October 14, 1941.

54. Davidman, "The Longest Way Round," p. 21.

55. *New Masses*, July 15, 1941.

56. *New Masses*, January 6, 1942.

57. On the performers listed, see reviews between 1941 and 1943 in *New Masses*, such as those of July 8, 1941; August 5, 1941; February 17, 1942; May 13, 1941. On "screwball comedy," see June 17, 1941.

58. HD to LD.

59. Pilat, "Girl Communist."

60. Ibid.

61. Davidman, "The Longest Way Round," pp. 21–22.

62. Ibid., p. 22.

63. Pilat, "Girl Communist."

64. Davidman, "The Longest Way Round," p. 22.

65. Thomas Yoseleff, ed., *Seven Poets in Search of an Answer* (New York: Bernard Ackerman, 1944).

66. My portrait of William Lindsay Gresham comes from things I learned from Chad Walsh to LD, Lake Iroquois, Vermont, July 23, 1981. Howard Davidman and Renée Gresham told me about him, too. Bill Gresham reveals much about his personality in "From Communist to Christian," in Soper, ed., *These Found the Way*, pp. 64–82.

67. Franklin Folsom to LD, May 30, 1982.

68. Gresham, "From Communist to Christian," pp. 71–72.

69. WLG to David Gresham, March 16, 1960.

70. DG to LD.

71. HD to LD.

72. *Poughkeepsie Sunday New Yorker*, June 6, 1948.

73. *New Masses*, July 31, 1945.

74. Helen Walker Puner to LD, November 29, 1981, and December 31, 1981.

75. Davidman, "The Longest Way Round," p. 23.

Chapter 3

1. Joy Davidman, "The Longest Way Round," in David Wesley Soper, ed., *These Found the Way: Thirteen Converts to Protestant Christianity* (Philadelphia: Westminster Press, 1951), p. 23.

2. Ibid.

3. Oliver Pilat, "Girl Communist," *New York Post*, October 31–November 13, 1949.

4. Davidman, "The Longest Way Round," p. 23.

5. Ibid., pp. 23–24.

6. Pilat, "Girl Communist."

7. Ibid.

8. Davidman, "The Longest Way Round," p. 24.

9. Ibid.

10. Ibid., pp. 24–25.

11. Ibid., p. 25; Pilat, "Girl Communist."

12. William Lindsay Gresham, *Nightmare Alley* (New York and Toronto, Ont.: Rinehart, 1946).

13. Gresham, "From Communist to Christian," in Soper, ed., *These Found the Way*, p. 65.

14. Bill wrote of his slaveowner ancestors in "From Communist to Christian," p. 65. A description of the grounds surrounding the house can be found in *Poughkeepsie Sunday New Yorker*, June 6, 1948.

15. Pilat, "Girl Communist."

16. Ibid.

17. RG to LD; Franklin Folsom to LD. May 30, 1982.

18. DG to LD.

19. Davidman, "The Longest Way Round," p. 24.

20. Francis Thompson, *The Hound of Heaven* (Wilton, Conn.: Morehouse-Barlow, 1980).

21. Davidman, "The Longest Way Round," p. 24.

22. Ibid., p. 25.

23. Ibid.

24. Ibid.; and Gresham, "From Communist to Christian," p. 82.

25. *The New York Times Book Review*, July 18, 1948.

26. *Atlantic Monthly* (September 1946).

27. Chad Walsh, *C. S. Lewis: Apostle to the Skeptics* (New York: Macmillan, 1949), Foreword, pp. ix–xi.

28. Pilat, "Girl Communist."

29. Chad and Eva Walsh granted me an interview at their summer home on Lake Iroquois, Vermont, July 23, 1981. Chad Walsh also made available to me copies of his correspondence with Joy Davidman.

30. Jacqueline Jackson to LD, July 23, 1981, Lake Iroquois, Vermont. For more information on Jackson, see Sheila Fitzgerald, "Profile: Jacqueline Jackson," in *Language Arts*, Vol. 58, no. 3 (March 1981), pp. 347–52.

31. William Lindsay Gresham, *Limbo Tower* (New York and Toronto, Ont.: Rinehart, 1949).

32. HD to LD; RG to LD.

33. Chad Walsh to LD.

34. Clyde S. Kilby and Marjorie Lamp Mead, eds., *Brothers and Friends: The Diaries of Major Warren Hamilton Lewis* (San Francisco: Harper & Row, 1982), p. 244.

35. JD to Chad Walsh, January 27, 1950.

36. Bill and Joy each contributed a chapter to Soper, ed., *These Found the Way*.

37. WLG to Davy (David Gresham), June 26, 1962.

38. JD to Chad Walsh, January 27, 1950.

39. WLG to Nancy, May 13, 1959.

40. DG to LD; HD to LD.

41. Chad Walsh to LD.

42. JD to Chad Walsh, February 27, 1953; RG to LD.

43. The material in the paragraph and the following ones comes from my interviews with Renée Gresham.

44. Jackie Jackson to LD, July 23, 1981. She told me that she saw Joy in Vermont and at Staatsburg and was impressed by how Joy loved the boys and paid close and loving attention to them.

45. JD to Renée Pierce, July 9, 1953, Joy Davidman Papers, Marion E. Wade Collection, Wheaton College, Wheaton, Illinois.

46. DG to LD.

47. HD to LD.

48. Pilat, "Girl Communist."

49. Herbert Aptheker to LD, May 21, 1981; Nina Schneider to LD, November 30, 1981.

50. HD to LD.

51. Soper, ed., *These Found the Way*, pp. 12–26. Quotation on p. 26.

52. Joy Davidman, *Weeping Bay* (New York: Macmillan, 1950), pp. 245–46.

53. *The New York Times*, March 5, 1950; *New York Herald Tribune Book Review*, March 12, 1950; *Catholic World*, June 1950; *Library Journal*, February 1, 1950. Excerpts from these and several other reviews are reprinted in *Book Review Digest*, 1950, pp. 227–28.

54. JD to Kenneth Porter, May 29, 1951.

55. Joy Davidman, *Smoke on the Mountain: An Interpretation of the Ten Commandments* (Philadelphia: Westminster Press, 1953, 1954).

56. Professor George Sayer to LD, August 7, 1981, Malvern, England.

57. Kilby and Mead, eds., *Brothers and Friends*, pp. 244–45.

58. George Sayer to LD.

59. Kilby and Mead, eds., *Brothers and Friends*, p. 244–45.

60. JD to Chad Walsh, January 25, 1953.

61. Walter Hooper, ed., *They Stand Together: The Letters of* C. S. *Lewis to Arthur Greeves* (1914–1963) (New York: Macmillan, 1979), p. 313.

62. WLG TO JD, n.d., 1952.

63. JD to Chad Walsh, February 27, 1953.

64. Kilby and Mead, eds., *Brothers and Friends*, p. 245.

65. RG to LD.

66. JD to Chad Walsh, February 27, 1953.

67. Ibid.

68. Ibid.

69. Chad Walsh to LD; RG to LD.

Chapter 4

1. DG to LD.
2. David Gresham to LD, September 16, 1981.
3. DG to LD.
4. JD to WLG, November 14, 1953.
5. JD to Chad Walsh, January 27, 1950.
6. George Sayer, who granted me a personal interview August 7, 1981, at Malvern, England, showed me a copy of C. S. Lewis's book, *A Preface to Paradise Lost*, rev. ed. (New York, London, and Toronto: Oxford University Press, 1952), which had belonged to Joy. She has written numerous marginal notes in the volume. On p. 102, where references are made to "Anger, hatred, blind fury . . ." Joy underwent some self-analysis and wrote, "My usual reaction, God help me!"
7. Joy Davidman, "The Longest Way Round," in David Wesley Soper, ed., *These Found the Way: Thirteen Converts to Protestant Christianity* (Philadelphia: Westminster Press, 1951), p 26.
8. JD to Chad Walsh, July 10, 1953.
9. JD to Kenneth Porter, August 18, 1951.
10. Ibid.
11. Oliver Pilat, "Girl Communist," *New York Post*, October 31–November 13, 1949.
12. JD to Chad Walsh, January 27, 1950.
13. Ibid.
14. Davidman, "The Longest Way Round," p. 26.
15. JD to WLG, November 19, 1953.
16. DG to LD.
17. David Gresham to LD, September 16, 1981; DG to LD.
18. JD to WLG, December 22, 1953.
19. Ibid.

20. C. S. Lewis to Vera Mathews Gebbert, December 23, 1953, Lewis Letters, Marion E. Wade Collection, Wheaton College, Wheaton, Illinois.

21. DG to LD.

22. Ibid.; JD to WLG, December 22, 1953.

23. JD to WLG, December 22, 1953.

24. George Sayer to LD; Sheldon Vanauken to LD, letter June 10, 1981, and phone interview June 19, 1981. The Reverend Walter Hooper was helpful to me on this subject when I interviewed him at Oxford on August 5, 1981.

25. HD to LD.

26. The correspondence between Joy and Bill is replete with evidence about the financial plight suffered on both sides of the Atlantic.

27. JD to WLG, April 2, 1954.

28. JD to WLG, June 2, 1955; May 23, 1955; February 8, 1955; March 16, 1955; JD to RG, May 23, 1955; and to WLG, April 29, 1955.

29. JD to WLG, May 10, 1954; March 16, 1955; August 28, 1955.

30. JD to WLG, October 22, 1954.

31. JD to WLG, October 29, 1954; April 15, 1955; JD to Chad Walsh, December 23, 1954.

32. JD to WLG, October 29, 1954; HD to LD.

33. JD to WLG. October 29, 1954.

34. Ibid.

35. Ibid.

36. JD to WLG, August 26, 1955; September 17, 1955; October 10, 1955.

37. DG to LD.

38. RG to LD; Bel Kaufman to LD, telephone interview, December 21, 1981.

39. Clyde S. Kilby and Marjorie Lamp Mead, eds., *Brothers and Friends: The Diaries of Major Warren Hamilton Lewis* (San Francisco: Harper & Row, 1982), p. 245.

40. Eva Walsh to LD, July 23, 1981.

41. W. H. Lewis, ed., *Letters of C. S. Lewis* (New York: Harcourt, Brace & World, 1966), p. 23.

42. C. S. Lewis, *A Grief Observed* (New York: Seabury Press, 1961), p. 8.

43. JD to WLG, November 30, 1954.

44. JD to WLG, April 29, 1955.

45. JD to WLG, March 16, 1955.

46. Joy recalled this in a letter to Bill, March 23, 1955.

47. JD to WLG, April 29, 1955.

48. Roger Lancelyn Green and Walter Hooper, *C. S. Lewis: A Biography* (New York and London: Harcourt Brace Jovanovich, 1974), p. 265.

49. Humphrey Carpenter, *The Inklings: C. S. Lewis, J. R. R. Tolkien, Charles Williams, and Their Friends* (Boston: Houghton Mifflin, 1979), p. 245.

50. Ibid.

51. George Sayer told me about this incident when I interviewed him at his home in Malvern, England, August 7, 1981.

52. C. S. Lewis, *Mere Christianity* (New York: Macmillan, 1956), pp. 81–88.

53. James T. Como., ed., *C. S. Lewis at the Breakfast Table and Other Reminiscences* (New York: Macmillan, 1979), p. 85.

54. George Sayer to LD; David Gresham to LD, September 16, 1981; Lewis, *A Grief Observed*, pp. 11, 38–39.

55. George Sayer to LD; DG to LD.

56. JD to WLG, December 21, 1955; December 31, 1955; DG to LD.

57. Kilby and Mead, eds., *Brothers and Friends*, p. 245.

58. Ibid.

59. The Reverend Peter W. Bide to LD, September 17, 1981.

60. JD to WLG, June 15, 1956.

61. JD to WLG, April 5 and May 2, 1956; see the acknowledgments of Warren H. Lewis, *Assault on Olympus: The Rise of the House of Gramont Between 1604 and 1678* (London: André Deutsch, 1958).

62. JD to WLG, October 19, 1956; JD to Chad and Eva Walsh, December 3, 1956.

63. JD to Chad and Eva Walsh, December 3, 1956; *The Times*, December 24, 1956, quoted in Walter Hooper, ed., *They Stand Together: The Letters of C. S. Lewis to Arthur Greeves* (1914–1963) (New York: Macmillan, 1979), p. 537.

64. JD to Chad and Eva Walsh, December 3, 1956.

65. Kilby and Mead, eds., *Brothers and Friends*, p. 245.

66. JD to Chad and Eva Walsh, December 3, 1956.

67. JD to Chad and Eva Walsh, February 5, 1957.

68. Ibid.

69. JD to Chad and Eva Walsh, February 8, 1957.

70. Kilby and Mead, eds., *Brothers and Friends*, p. 245; Sheldon Vanauken, *A Severe Mercy* (San Francisco: Harper & Row, 1977), pp. 227–28.

71. The Reverend Peter W. Bide to LD, September 17, 1981.

72. Kilby and Mead, eds., *Brothers and Friends*, p. 246.

73. Nevill Coghill, "The Approach to English," in Joycelyn Gibb, ed., *Light on C. S. Lewis* (New York: Harcourt, Brace & World, 1966), p. 63.

74. Vanauken, *A Severe Mercy*, pp. 227–28.

75. C. S. Lewis to Sister Penelope, May 12, 1957, Lewis Letters, Marion E. Wade Collection, Wheaton College, Wheaton, Illinois.

76. Ibid., March 6, 1957.

77. C. S. Lewis to Dom Bede Griffiths, August 1, 1957, Lewis Letters, Marion E. Wade Collection, Wheaton College, Wheaton, Illinois.

78. Bel Kaufman sent me copies of her diary dated August 25, 26, 27, 1957. I interviewed Ms. Kaufman on the telephone December 22, 1981, and she wrote a lengthy letter of reminiscences dated December 5, 1981.

79. C. S. Lewis to Dom Bede Griffiths, September 24, 1957, Lewis Letters, Marion E. Wade Collection, Wheaton College, Wheaton, Illinois; JD to WLG, October 31, 1957.

80. JD to WLG, November 29, 1957; C. S. Lewis to Sister Penelope, November 6, 1957, Lewis Letters, Marion E. Wade Collection, Wheaton College, Wheaton, Illinois.

81. Lewis, ed., *Letters of C. S. Lewis*, "Memoir of C. S. Lewis," p. 22.

82. Joy's correspondence with Bill contains many references to Warren Lewis's alcoholism. See, for example, January 8 and December 7, 1956. Warren gives some insight into his wrestlings with the problem in his diaries. See, for example, p. 253 of Kilby and Mead, eds., *Brothers and Friends.*

83. Joy Lewis to Mary, June 6, 1958, quoted in Clyde S. Kilby, ed., *C. S. Lewis: Letters to an American Lady* (Grand Rapids, Mich.: William B. Eerdmans, 1967), pp. 72–74.

84. Warren H. Lewis, *The Scandalous Regent: A Life of Philippe, Duc d'Orleans, 1674–1723, and of His Family* (London: André Deutsch, 1961).

85. JD to WLG, February 4, 1958.

86. George Sayer to LD; DG to LD; Chad and Eva Walsh to LD.

87. Kilby and Mead, eds., *Brothers and Friends*, pp. 60–61.

88. JD to WLG, July 14, 1958.

89. Ibid.

90. WLG to JD, April 2, 1957.

91. C. S. Lewis to WLG, April 6, 1957. Marion E. Wade Collection, Wheaton College, Wheaton, Illinois.

92. DG to LD.

93. Ibid.

94. C. S. Lewis to Mary, April 15, 1958, quoted in Kilby, ed., *Letters to an American Lady*, p. 72.

95. Lewis, *A Grief Observed*, p. 39.

96. C. S. Lewis, *The Four Loves* (New York: Harcourt Brace Jovanovich, 1960), p. 154; C. S. Lewis to Sister Penelope, February 12, 1958, Marion E. Wade Collection, Wheaton College, Wheaton. Illinois.

97. JD to WLG, August 8, 1959. There is mention of the Lewises' visit with Arthur Greeves in Hooper, ed., *They Stand Together*, p. 552.

98. JD to WLG, September 26, 1959.

99. Ibid.

100. C. S. Lewis to Sister Penelope, November 6, 1957.

101. C. S. Lewis to Mary, October 18, 1959, quoted in Kilby, ed., *Letters to an American Lady*, p. 85.

102. JD to WLG, December 15, 1959.

103. JD to WLG, March 30, 1960.

104. C. S. Lewis to Mary, April 19, 1960, quoted in Kilby, ed., *Letters to an American Lady*, p. 88.

105. This quotation appears in a footnote on p. 553 of Hooper, ed., *They Stand Together*.

106. JD to WLG, March 30, 1960.

107. Notes from Warren H. Lewis's diary, in the Joy Davidman File, Marion E. Wade Collection, Wheaton College, Wheaton, Illinois.

108. Joy Davidman File, Marion E. Wade Collection, Wheaton College, Wheaton, Illinois; JD to WLG, June 27,

July 2, 1960; Kilby and Mead, eds., *Brothers and Friends*,
p. 248.

109. Kilby and Mead, eds., *Brothers and Friends*, p. 248.
110. Ibid., p. 249.
111. Lewis, *A Grief Observed*, p. 59.
112. Kilby and Mead, eds., *Brothers and Friends*, p. 250.
113. Ibid.
114. Ibid.; C. S. Lewis, *A Grief Observed*, p. 60.

Chapter 5

1. Clyde S. Kilby and Marjorie Lamp Mead, eds., *Brothers and Friends: The Diaries of Major Warren Hamilton Lewis* (San Francisco: Harper & Row, 1982), pp. 250–51 contain some details about the weather and those going to the funeral.
2. Ibid., p. 250 describes the weather.
3. Ibid.
4. JD to Kenneth Porter, August 18, 1951.
5. Kilby and Mead, eds., *Brothers and Friends*, p. 251.
6. C. S. Lewis, *A Grief Observed* (New York: Seabury Press, 1961), pp. 57–58.
7. Humphrey Carpenter, *The Inklings: C. S. Lewis, J. R. R. Tolkien, Charles Williams, and Their Friends* (Boston: Houghton Mifflin, 1979), pp. 216–17.
8. Roger Lancelyn Green and Walter Hooper, *C. S. Lewis: A Biography* (New York and London: Harcourt Brace Jovanovich, 1974), p. 267.
9. Joy Davidman, *Smoke on the Mountain: An Interpretation of the Ten Commandments* (Philadelphia: Westminster Press, 1953).

Index

AND GOD CAME IN

Text scanned by Scribe, Philadelphia, PA (scribenet.com).

The text of this book is set in Dante, Requiem,
and Type Embellishments Three.

Typeset in Quark XPress.

Interior design and typesetting by
Rose Yancik • Y Design